BUYING, SELLING & MERGING A MEDICAL PRACTICE

Proven Valuation and Negotiation Strategies

KENNETH M. HEKMAN

IRWIN
Professional Publishing®
Chicago • London • Singapore

◥▀▶ **Times Mirror**
◣◢ **Higher Education Group**

Library of Congress Cataloging-in-Publication Data

Hekman, Kenneth M.
  Buying, selling, and merging medical practices: how to structure, negotiate, and implement transactions for long-term success / Kenneth M. Hekman.
    p. cm.
  Includes bibliographical references and index.
  ISBN 0-7863-0815-X
    1. Medicine—Practice—Accounting. 2. Medicine—Practice—
  —Economic aspects. 3. Business enterprises—Valuation. I. Title.
  HF5686.P37H45 1996
  362.1'01681—dc20   96–17364

Printed in the United States of America
1 2 3 4 5 6 7 8 9 0 3 2 1 0 9 8 7 6

PREFACE

In December 1995, the *American Medical News* reported that 36 percent of hospitals have bought medical practices during the last five years. But only 17 percent of those who acquired practices reported generating positive returns on their investments. What went wrong? How can integrated health systems hope to deliver care more efficiently in the face of persistent losses?

Buying, Selling & Merging A Medical Practice is geared toward helping physicians and hospital executives form win–win relationships. It offers reminders of the business principles fundamental to successful partnerships, tailoring those concepts to the medical practice environment. The key role of an independent appraisal is explained and demonstrated to produce more successful deal-making. Those who learn from its simple message can avoid expensive lessons and form long-lasting business relationships that effectively bring healthcare to people who need it most.

The importance of an independent appraisal is affirmed by the Internal Revenue Service. Their concern about fair market valuations of practice assets has led to the inclusion of the following language in favorable exemption letters related to hospitals' 501(c)(3) status:

"Applicant represents that all assets acquired will be at or below Fair Market Value (FMV) and will be the result of independent appraisals and arms-length negotiation." (Kaiser, Haney and Sullivan, 1994)

This book offers perspectives from several disciplines. The early chapters describe the art and science of business appraisals, including the introduction of a derivative technique uniquely designed for measuring the business value of medical practices. The author's point of view is that of an insider. He has worked as a medical group administrator and business consultant to hundreds of physicians in a broad spectrum of specialties. But the book is also sensitive to the dynamics of the hospital executive's environment. The role of the health systems management team is to manage change, including the challenge of blending unlike corporate cultures.

Some of the nuances of contracts and negotiations are the focus of the middle chapters. And whatever you do, don't skip Chapter 10. The vision for life after the deal offered in this chapter gives an overall context in which to view the appraisal and negotiation process.

Those considering merging rather than selling will find the material equally beneficial. In some respects, merging *is* selling. It is selling and buying at the same time. The principles that apply to valuation are quite translatable to mergers, and the insights about life after the deal are all the more applicable.

Enjoy the book. It is more than a technical guide. Think of it as a coach in the integration game. Look for its wisdom as well as its methods.

TABLE OF CONTENTS

Chapter 3

Traditional Methods for Measuring the Value of Intangibles (Goodwill) 31

Chapter 4

New Traditions in Goodwill Measurement 45

Appendex to Chapter 4

Boondocks Family Health Center Practice Appraisal 57

1
CHAPTER

Understanding Valuation Concepts

WHAT IS AN APPRAISAL?

How do you determine the value of a medical practice? How do you develop an understanding of the value of anything? The first right answer is, through negotiation. Consider your role as the buyer of a piece of property such as a house or a car. You find a willing seller and you consider the benefits and features of his particular piece of property. Then you negotiate; you haggle, you figure out what the central points of agreement might be. You work to overcome the objections of the seller and convince him of the essential correctness of your own assertions.

Negotiating is part of the process in medical practice acquisitions as well, but there is more at stake in most of these transactions. The community's interest is at risk when medical service delivery systems are being adjusted. The complexity and long-term significance of the transaction calls for more than simple negotiation between the buyer and the seller. That is why I advocate a discovery process to supplement the negotiations, and open communication about the facts to equalize the negotiating positions for an outcome that serves the public interest. That discovery process is the essence of an appraisal.

An independent appraisal allows the buyer and the seller to look at the components of value—the tangible values and the intangible values—and come to a logical understanding about how each component contributes to the business success of the proposed transaction. The appraisal does not assume that both parties will necessarily agree about the value of each component. The purpose of the appraisal is to place the issues on the negotiating table, with supporting information, to enable both parties to come to a more complete understanding of how a win–win situation can be structured.

Appraisals expose the value of a medical practice at a particular point in time, but they can also show owners how to improve the value of the practice. The purpose of any transaction should be to improve the value of medical services offered to the community. An acquisition or merger can do that in four major ways:

1. The new entity can enable physicians to boost their productivity through better incentives, more efficient support systems, access to procedural capabilities they would not have without the acquisition, or any other specific ways.

2. The new entity might provide ways to cut costs through group purchasing; cross-trained staff, which can reduce overhead; better utilization of high-cost facilities and equipment; and skilled management.

3. The new entity may add value to the patient–physician relationship in ways the former structure could not. The value of a medical practice might be increased by adding specialty services to primary care so that patients can make a one-stop visit to a single facility to get most of the services they need. Or value may be increased by adding primary care physicians to a group of specialists. The larger group may be able to integrate capital-intensive services, such as lab and X-ray, that each group could not justify on its own.

4. The new entity may also add value by giving the new venture greater negotiating strength than either party may have had prior to the transaction. This is the driving force behind many medical practice acquisitions. It is based on the belief that preserving market share while dealing with managed care entities will require the negotiating strength that comes only from large and efficient medical care delivery systems.

Merged companies often look for new ways to find economies of scale in operations. As medical groups become more capable of refining their information systems, securing skilled management, and attracting larger shares of the limited pool of patients, organizations may be able to provide services at lower total cost and increase their attractiveness to the managed care organizations. An appraisal can expose the potential new values that may result from the proposed transaction as well as measure the components of value of the practices as they stand prior to the transaction. Identifying the future value can be a key to understanding the present value of the medical practice.

Determining Economic Value

These benefits of a potential medical practice acquisition are sometimes referred to as the components of economic value. The role of the appraiser is to find the economic value of a business as distinguished from the simple book value. Ray Miles describes economic value as "that kind of value according to which a thing is capable of producing economic benefits for its owner or user."[1]

The economic benefits of a medical practice are of central importance to buyers and sellers in a variety of circumstances. They are crucial in establishing a price when the practice passes from one physician to another in the

---

1. Raymond C. Miles, *Basic Business Appraisal,* Southeast Business Investment Corp., 1984, p. 16.

simplest of sales. The economic benefits are the foundation for a merger of two or more groups into a single organization. Hospitals and insurance companies that acquire medical practices are looking for the economic benefits of controlling an integrated delivery system. In short, if there is not a compelling economic reason to consider a transaction, the deal is without purpose.

How Economic Value Differs from Book Value

Determining the value of a medical practice might be easy if the buyer and seller could simply look at the balance sheet and agree on the equity in the business. But there are several difficulties with relying on the balance sheet alone and basing the value of the business on the book value. The purpose of the balance sheet is to give the owner of the business information about the financial soundness of the operations. The process of preparing a balance sheet is determined by following the rules established by the Internal Revenue Service (IRS) and in accordance with generally accepted accounting principles.

Buyers and sellers are not so concerned with the expectations of the IRS and the accounting disciplines. They are looking for the economic benefits of owning the business. Balance sheets are typically silent on some of those benefits, and may understate or overstate some other critical components of the business. For example, cash-basis accounting, which most professional corporations adhere to, does not require the balance sheet to include accounts receivable. Goodwill is usually excluded from the balance sheet unless the current owner has paid a previous owner an amount in excess of the tangible assets. Chapter 2 will expand on the differences between the book value and the economic value, but the point is that the balance sheet must be restated to show the economic value of the business.

Types of Economic Value

The difficulty of measuring the economic benefits of a business can be compounded by the multiplicity of terms and concepts that people use in referring to value. Some of the subtypes, or standards, of economic value referred to by buyers and sellers include:

Fair market value	Liquidation value
Going concern value	Intrinsic value
Investment value	Replacement value
Goodwill value	Insurable value

There are also values that people place on property that might be considered noneconomic values. An owner might assign a value to an object or business that reflects the owner's attachment or affection for the entity, but this value may have no bearing on its economic benefits to the owner. For example, I have an old outdoor thermometer that advertises the business my father owned when I was a child. Its value to anyone outside my family is probably zero, but I assign sentimental value to it that would make it very difficult for me to sell at any price. Many physicians find themselves in similar positions of affection toward their practices. They may have spent the bulk of their career caring intimately for patients who have become trusted friends. Measuring the value of such a medical practice in a way that matches the personal value to the physician is unreasonable. Before an appraisal can lead to a successful conclusion about the business value, the buyer and seller need to agree on the standard of value that will be used.

Separating Personal Goodwill from Corporate Goodwill

A critical function of a medical practice appraisal is to help the buyer and the seller to segregate the value of the business that is intrinsic to the practitioner from the value of the business that is transferable. The caring tradition, bedside manner, and charisma of an individual physician may have contributed a great deal to the profitability of his or her practice, but these characteristics are not transferable to another physician simply by virtue of a negotiated transaction.

Business characteristics that are transferable include such things as an attractive setting, strong payer mix, effective systems for billing and collections, productive managed care contracts, and a large volume of satisfied patients. These are corporate goodwill factors that can form the foundation for long-term business success. They can be highly valuable if they translate to strong future revenues, strategic marketing advantages, or lower operating costs systemwide for the acquiring organization.

Business Valuation Standards

The appraisal discipline is relatively young, compared to other professions. The development of business valuation standards is proceeding gradually through IRS rulings, litigation, professional certification processes, and associations of appraisers.

IRS Revenue Rulings   Two critical revenue rulings by the Internal Revenue Service have formed a foundation for the development of standards in the appraisal disciplines. Revenue Ruling 59-60 outlines, in general terms, ways to approach the valuation process and factors to consider when valuing closely held stock. Revenue Ruling 68-609 describes a formula that is generally referred to as a capitalization of excess earnings formula. The IRS does not imply with these rulings that there are a limited number of correct ways to value a business. On the contrary, Revenue Ruling 68-609 states: "The 'formula' approach should not be used if there is better evidence available from which the value of intangibles can be determined." Appendixes A and B present these two foundational revenue rulings.

Uniform Standards of Professional Appraisal Practice (USPAP)   In 1987, nine of the leading professional appraisal associations in the United States adopted a landmark document titled "Uniform Standards of Professional Appraisal Practice (USPAP)." The standards were produced by the Appraisal Foundation, which monitors developments in the field and provides continuous improvements to the standards. The first 6 of the 10 standards deal with real estate appraisal. Standards 7 and 8 deal with personal property appraisal. Standards 9 and 10 of the USPAP focus on the expectations for business valuations conducted by professional appraisers.

Certification of Appraisers There are two prominent professional associations to serve the appraisal community, each with their own credentialing curricula. The American Society of Appraisers (ASA) offers accreditation designations in four areas of interest. Individuals who have attained requisite levels of education and experience, and who adhere to strict ethical and professional standards, may hold one or more professional designations in the ASA. The areas of interest are business valuation, machinery and technical specialties, personal property, and real property.[2]

The Institute of Business Appraisers, Inc., concentrates on the professional development of specialists in business valuation. Members can earn the designation of Certified Business Appraiser (CBA) through testing and submission of a series of case studies. The professional association also maintains a database of transactions involving medical practice acquisitions nationwide.[3]

DETERMINING WHAT YOU ARE BUYING OR SELLING

The first step in developing a transaction is to determine what is being bought or sold. This may sound elementary, but the answer is not always as obvious as it may seem. A

---

2. The American Society of Appraisers address is P.O. Box 17265, Washington, D.C. 20041. Phone: 703-478-2228.
3. The Institute of Business Appraisers address is P.O. Box 1447, Boynton Beach, FL 33425. Phone: 407-732-3202.

physician who intends to retire has less to offer for sale than a midcareer physician who intends to maintain the practice as an employee of the new owner. Likewise, a thriving practice that is burdened by debt falls short of its optimal value unless the debts are segregated and excluded from the transaction.

There are four basic components of the business to consider when the buyer and the seller consider a transaction. Three of these components—assets, liabilities, and equity—are reflected in the balance sheet, although they may require adjustment or interpretation to reflect a fair conclusion. The fourth component is goodwill, which is usually not a part of the balance sheet but can become a significant part of the transaction.

Tangible Assets

Tangible assets are the items of equipment, cash, accounts receivable, and other property that are owned by the practice. The current value of each component may vary widely from its original value. It may be either higher or lower than the balance sheet indicates. Chapter 2 deals with valuation techniques for tangible assets in greater detail.

In most transactions, the cash is excluded from the valuation on the assumption that the sellers will distribute excess cash among themselves prior to the transaction, just as they would at their fiscal year-end to avoid corporate taxes.

Accounts receivable may or may not be included in the transaction. Acquiring receivables at their collectable value may help the buyer maintain an even cash flow in the initial stage of ownership, and make for a complete break from the business for the seller. But receivables may not be worth as much in the mind of the buyer as they are in the eyes of the seller, and the buyer may have greater difficulty collecting receivables owned by patients who feel no loyalty or obligation once the former practitioner is no longer involved. If receivables are retained by the seller, he or she may want to either collect them independently, or ask the buyer to collect them, retain a service fee, and forward the remainder to the seller over a period of three to six months.

The value of the equipment may be quite different from the amounts indicated on the balance sheet. The practice may have taken accelerated depreciation as allowed by the Internal Revenue Service, driving the balance sheet value far below the original cost. But the equipment may have an extensive remaining useful life. It may be more valuable to the buyer than the depreciated value represents because the equipment is familiar and comfortable to the practitioners, and it may represent a bargain at fair market value compared to the alternative of purchasing all new equipment.

The asset section of the balance sheet may exclude certain items that should be recognized through the appraisal process. For example, a professional liability insurance premium may be paid a year in advance, representing remaining value to the seller at the time of a midyear transaction. The unused portion of the premium might be refunded to the seller if he or she does not intend to continue in employment with the buyer, or the value of the unused premium can be included in the appraised value of the assets and recognized in the transaction price.

Liabilities

Liabilities are debts that the practice has incurred and for which there is a future obligation to pay. They may be loans that are secured by real property, life insurance, equipment, or accounts receivable. They may also include unsecured debts, money that was loaned to the practice on the personal guarantee of the physicians. The money may have been used to acquire specific assets or to maintain cash flow through uneven periods. Each liability on the balance sheet should be negotiated separately to determine the net value of the business in its unencumbered state.

Some liabilities may not appear on the balance sheet but should be exposed through the appraisal process. They may include obligations such as unfunded employee vacation time, overdue bills, unpaid taxes, loans to shareholders, or obligations to former shareholders who are being bought out.

Equity

Equity is the difference between what a practice owns (assets) and what it owes (liabilities). Equity represents what the practice owns free and clear. It is the residual value of stock and retained earnings.

Since equity is the value of stock, it is included in the transaction only when the business is being acquired in its entirety, typically when physicians sell to other physicians. Most medical practices are operated as professional corporations or professional associations in which the shareholders must be licensed practitioners. A hospital or insurance company cannot legally acquire the stock of a professional corporation, so they will exclude stock *per se* from the appraisal. That is not to say, however, that the concept of stock ownership has no value to these buyers. It simply indicates that nonphysician buyers must secure the future cash flow of the business through fair dealings on tangible assets, value for goodwill, and sound employment practices after the transaction.

Intangible Assets

Intangible assets include all the characteristics that contribute to the business success of the medical practice. They are often referred to collectively as "goodwill" or "going concern value." They may include such things as the reputation of the physicians, the location of the practice, the loyalty and volume of high-paying patients, and the management systems that contribute to low overhead costs.

Few topics create as much controversy as the place of goodwill in acquiring medical practices. Many hospitals have sought to maintain a firm policy of not paying for goodwill, but market forces have challenged their assumptions and altered their stance. Conversely, many physicians have built their practices around the assumption that their goodwill would serve as the foundation of their retirement plan. They practiced diligently for decades in the expectation that a younger physician would be ready to buy the practice at full value when it was time to bow out. The tension of these two perspectives is coming into full view with the development of managed care and the need for integrated systems. Indeed, the core purpose of this book is to guide buyers and sellers through that tension and to develop stronger medical delivery systems as a result of it.

THREE APPROACHES TO MEASURING BUSINESS VALUE

The business valuation methods for medical practices fall under three general categories: asset-based valuation, income-based valuation, and market valuation.

Asset-Based Valuation

Asset-based valuation begins with the construction of an adjusted balance sheet. The appraiser looks at the organization at a particular point in time and determines the book value of the business at this point. In a merger, the adjusted balance sheets of both organizations are compared to determine the relative contribution to fair market value of each entity. The appraiser determines the value of the supplies, the equipment, the accounts receivable, the cash, and the real estate.

The asset-based valuation should also examine and determine the value of intangible assets. The intangible value may be determined by measuring seemingly unmeasurable factors such as reputation, name recognition, location, and telephone number. The valuation of intangibles has become one of the most difficult and problematic barriers to reaching fair values in medical practice transactions, and for good reasons. The nature of these intangible assets is like air. The observer cannot see them directly; only the evidence of their presence can be measured. Intangible assets are surrounded by emotional and ego attachments and are heavily influenced by human perspectives. Their value depends largely on the observer's point of view: The seller is likely to assign a higher value to the intangibles than the buyer. In the sensitivity about intangibles, both parties find themselves walking lightly so as not to offend the other or to spoil a deal that may be in both parties' long-term interests.

Because of the sensitivity and elusiveness of measuring intangible assets directly, appraisers have developed a variety of surrogate measures. The value of goodwill may be more consistently and logically determined by examining its effect on profitability and cash flow. Asset-based techniques are therefore usually confined to the measurement of tangible assets. The values assigned to the tangible assets may be combined with certain measurements of intangibles to yield a complete picture of the value of the medical practice as a business. The combination of a market valuation of tangible assets and a market valuation of intangibles through the use of the excess earnings method will be examined in Chapter 3.

Income-Based Valuation

The second general classification is the income-based valuation, in which the appraiser looks at the historical revenue stream and the projected revenue streams to come to an understanding of value on the basis of future benefits. The net present value of those future benefits can become the basis for an understanding of the fair market value of both tangible and intangible assets. The method is most applicable when it is clear that the new entity has an opportunity to gain improved revenues because of increasing productivity, decreasing costs, or other major value-adding features. The analytical process for determining value through a review of the revenue stream is similar to that which a banker might undertake to ensure that a borrower is creditworthy. The revenue stream must be sufficient to repay the loan tendered by the bank. Likewise, the revenue stream must be sufficient to provide a return on investment to the buyer of a medical practice.

Market Valuation

The third general classification of appraisal techniques is market valuation. It may be built upon the first two approaches, but it goes beyond the asset-based approach and the income-based approach and asks, What is the market willing to pay? The market value may vary widely from the values determined by other techniques. Regardless of what the property is worth, and regardless of how successful it has been, if there is competition for a medical practice, the market value might be considerably different than if this is a very quiet, single transaction occurring between one buyer and one seller. The market dynamics can change the value of a transaction markedly. This principle is true for the whole organization, and it is equally true for some of its parts.

The wild fluctuations in prices paid for medical practices in the past decade have most likely been fueled by the growing competition for physicians and their patients. Market valuation methods have

RULES OF THUMB

Rules of thumb may have been sufficient for determining the value of a medical practice in the past, but they are probably not adequate in today's market.

One of the most common rules of thumb is to base the value of goodwill on a percent of the last year's revenue. The method still has some validity but there can be wide variations in how it is used. It is appealing in its simplicity, but its conclusions may have no connection with other, more logical valuation processes.

Another rule of thumb that surfaces periodically bases the intangible value of a

(Continued)

prevailed in some medical practice acquisitions, with resulting prices so high that the buyers cannot ever expect to achieve a return on their investment, even through indirect revenue streams. When this happens, I believe the public interest is harmed. Institutions that pay too much seek ways to pass those costs on to their consumers, decreasing the institution's competitiveness. Physicians who experience a windfall are more likely to lose interest in using their talents for the benefit of their patients. And the precedent for similar transactions in the community only exacerbates the problem for institutions, physicians, and patients.

VALUATION THEORY AND CONCEPTS

Measuring the economic benefits of business ownership requires a brief review of valuation theory.

Fair Market Value

Fair market value is a core type of economic value. "*Fair market value* is the price, in cash or equivalent, that a buyer could *reasonably* be expected to pay, and a seller could *reasonably* be expected to accept, if the property were

practice on a certain rate per chart. Those rules of thumb may have worked in friendly transactions in the past. The typical scenario is that a new physician is recruited to a group. She is there for a year or two before she is given the opportunity to buy in. The group already likes her, and she likes them. They have already agreed on the concept of the buy-in and merely need to agree on the specifics. So a very friendly, casual, simplistic method for determining the value at that point may be adequate. The circumstances of that buy-in are not really market driven.

These rules of thumb may have been adequate in the past, and they may still be adequate in some circumstances, but in a highly competitive market, we are going to find that rules of thumb are no longer adequate substitutes for a disciplined approach to valuation.

exposed for sale on the *open market* for a *reasonable period of time,* with both buyer and seller being in *possession of the pertinent facts,* and neither being under *compulsion to act.*"[4]

This definition may be considered quite complete, but it presents enormous challenges to the medical practice appraiser. How is "reasonably" defined? Ultimately it can be determined only by the buyer and the seller. The appraisal process can assist with insights about existing values, the potential for new value that might be added through the proposed transaction, and the value of similar transactions recently negotiated in the community. But the jury that defines reasonableness is not composed of a dozen peers as in the justice system. In these transactions, the jury is relatively small and consists largely of participants in the transaction.

Is there an open market? Medical practices can't be purchased by just anyone and can't be expected to continue the revenue stream without a physician. Only a licensed physician can provide the revenue stream the purchaser of a practice can hope to control. That is not exactly an open market in the same sense that a financially qualified person could own a restaurant or a hardware store.

What is a reasonable period of time? The details of most medical practice offerings are not widely known until the sale is announced. The secrecy is necessary to protect the predictability of the patient flow, which is at the heart of the business value. Secrecy precludes both open markets and reasonable time for the offering to be communicated to multiple potential buyers.

What are the pertinent facts and who has possession of them? In most traditional buying relationships, the facts are not well known by either party. The traditional transaction is often based on mutual trust, even to the point of ignoring or not paying attention to the overhead, the management, the marketing tactics and strategy, or any long-term planning. If the pertinent facts are known, they are

---

4. Raymond C. Miles, ibid. p. 19, emphases mine.

most likely to be in the possession of the seller, giving him or her an unfair advantage in negotiating the fair market value. If the buyer elects to conduct an appraisal by hiring an outside consultant, the buyer may have more knowledge of the pertinent facts than the seller.

What does it mean not to be under compulsion to act? In my experience, there are few cases of proposed medical practice sales where there is a compulsion to sell, but there is often a sense of urgency. Some physicians are panicking. They are begging to be bought out before the expected reimbursement cuts threaten their incomes significantly. Hospitals likewise are frequently acting out of anxiety. Some are compelled to purchase the practices of their loyal admitters before their crosstown rival hospital dangles a large bag of money under the physicians' noses to entice them into their fold. Many a hospital administrator has become a reluctant owner of medical practices, only to find out they don't perform like other clinical departments. That urgency is about as close as a compulsion to act as I can imagine under the current market.

The problems associated with finding a fair market value are myriad. We can't define "reasonable" very clearly. We can't identify an open market well. We don't know how to identify a reasonable period of time or possession of pertinent facts. And the compulsion to act seems to be a frequent condition. These are significant problems that impact our understanding of the fair market value of medical practices. The traditional valuation methods offer little assistance in solving these problems, but the techniques described in Chapter 3 are designed to overcome their limitations and to advance the art of the appraisal.

Highest and Best Use

I recently appraised a practice that was absolutely astounding. A solo practice physician was seeing an average of 80 patients a day, a volume unrivaled by his peers. My interest in his efficiency and drive was piqued. I found that the man drove himself to a point of dysfunction, which forced the liquidation of his practice. He exceeded the reasonably feasible present use of the practice assets. It is unreasonable to expect that another physician can buy the practice and continue the volume and profitability enjoyed by his predecessor. It is actually a practice of sufficient size to be sustained by two or three physicians.

The highest and best use of a medical practice's assets may not be to sustain the practice as it is currently functioning. A practice may have assets that are dormant or not being used to their fullest potential. An X-ray machine might be available but seldom used in a small office, for example. If the unit is relatively new and in good condition, its highest and best use might be to sell it rather than to expend its limited cash flow on maintenance and perishable supplies. Keeping it may also risk less-than-optimal medical judgments based on its infrequent use by an inadequately trained technician. On the other hand, the unit's highest and best use might be better realized if the practice can be sold or merged with other physicians who could increase its use for profitable and medically justified services.

The principle of seeking the highest and best use of assets can apply to people as well as to equipment. The appraisal process might reveal that a physician has a secret desire to pursue an interest in developing a new procedural capability. Perhaps that interest entails a capital expenditure that the physician is unwilling to make under his or her current business structure, but that is both feasible and desirable under the proposed structure. The future value of that new line of business is material to the appraisal, since it represents a higher and better use of the physician's talents and interests.

Principle of Alternatives

The principle of alternatives declares that in any contemplated transaction, each party has alternatives to consummating the transaction. If there are not alternatives for both buyer and seller, the fair market value is much more difficult to determine. A hospital could buy a similar practice that is a competitor to the one under consideration. The physicians may be willing to work with other hospitals, and the fact that that option is a reasonable alternative lends greater validity to an assessment of the fair market value for the practice.

Principle of Substitution

The principle of substitution simply says that the value of a thing tends to be determined by the cost of acquiring an equally desirable substitute. For buyers, that includes the substitute of acquiring an alternative competitor or the substitute of starting a new practice from scratch. An institution can recruit physicians, set them up in practice, and develop a competitor rather than buying a going concern. Analyzing the cost of developing a substitute can provide insights into the economic value of acquiring an existing practice.

Principle of Future Benefits

Finally, the principle of future benefits states that economic value reflects anticipated future benefits. The buyer must believe that she will realize an advantage by purchasing the business that she would not otherwise have. That belief may be based on projections of future cash flows, plans for lowering costs, negotiating leverage that might be gained by combining forces, or some other anticipated strategic advantage.

THE ROLE OF THE APPRAISER

The professional medical practice appraiser can play a vital role in setting the stage for a win–win transaction. To be effective, the appraiser must be independent of both parties, and the professional fee earned must not be related to the conclusion of value. But both parties stand to gain from a sound appraisal, since it helps them understand the economic benefit of settling at a specific value.

The buyer benefits from the appraisal process by gaining inside information about the practice from a critical evaluation of the financial performance and market position. The appraisal report may contain vital information that can become the basis of the due diligence process. The appraiser's conclusion of value may help the buyer convince the seller to segregate personal values from economic values, and create a more realistic environment for win–win negotiations.

The seller benefits from the appraisal process by obtaining an independent, documented opinion to support the physician's intuitive case for business value. The appraisal techniques reveal the effects of hundreds of business decisions made by the seller over years of practice. They can either affirm the wisdom of those decisions or point to corrective actions to boost future business value. A well-written report can document the components of value in a way that might be impossible for the practitioner who views his or her business with the pride of ownership.

Business appraisers typically come from backgrounds in accounting, law, or marketing/consulting. Each discipline brings its own wealth of perspectives to bear on the appraisal assignment. Accountants may bring a helpful perspective on the intrinsic value of stock, and attorneys might approach the assignment with a view toward protecting the buyer and seller from illegal combinations. My own perspective as a consultant is based on more than 20 years as a healthcare executive. My education and experience has afforded me the opportunity to conduct sound financial analyses coupled with an eye toward improving the value after the transaction.

2
CHAPTER

Measuring the Value of Tangibles

WHEN TANGIBLES ARE IMPORTANT IN THE VALUATION PROCESS

Tangible items may be the most visible component of a proposed transaction, but they may not be the most valuable. A physical inventory of all equipment and supplies may be necessary in some transactions, but unnecessary in others. In all cases, however, the appraisal should include a restatement of the balance sheet to recognize the economic value of the business, in contrast to the book value.

Asset-Only Transactions

A complete inventory of equipment and supplies is the core component of value when the appraisal assignment is for hard assets only. An example of an asset-only transaction might be the purchase of a practice that is owned by a retiring physician. His intention may be to liquidate his remaining assets and encourage his patients to seek continuing care elsewhere. A disabled physician may be in a similar position, as would a physician who is electing to return to a residency or move away for other reasons. The asset-only transaction might also occur if an institution is acquiring practices without competition from other institutions. Physicians in some communities may be willing to sell for the value of their tangible assets only, simply to escape from the pressures of managing their practice or the uncertainties of reimbursement.

In Combination with Excess Earnings Method

The value of tangibles is also critical when it is combined with a particular income-based method for measuring goodwill known as the excess earnings technique. The excess earnings method will be described in Chapter 3. The reason why assets are added to the results of the excess earnings method is that the goodwill measurement resulting from the excess earnings method is based on a part of the revenue stream rather on than the entire cash flow of the business. The method is designed to capture only the portion of profits that results from intangible assets, which must then be added to the value of tangible assets to yield a complete picture of the value of the practice.

MEASUREMENT METHODS

Depreciated Value

The balance sheet typically documents the amount paid for tangible assets such as equipment and real property, with a separate line to identify the accumulated depreciation taken thus far in the life of the assets. The rules for determining the allowable depreciation are established by the Internal Revenue Service. Depreciation is allowed as an expense to recognize that equipment wears out, to encourage businesses to invest in productivity-boosting capital equipment, and to maintain up-to-date support systems.

The rules for depreciation are generally favorable for businesses. They allow the original value of equipment to be expensed more rapidly than the equipment is likely to wear. Many items of office equipment can be depreciated over a five-year period, while others are granted a seven-year depreciable life. The rules for depreciation also allow for acceleration of the allowed expense such that greater portions of the depreciation expense can be recognized in the early years of ownership. Section 179 of the revenue code also allows for the complete write-off of equipment up to a specified level each year.

The impact of the depreciation rules is that the net value of tangible assets on the balance sheet, after accumulated depreciation, is frequently less than the money-making usefulness of those assets. Equipment that may have a realistic life of 15 or 20 years may be fully depreciated by the time it is 7 years old. Conversely, computer equipment that may be obsolete might still have book value if it is being depreciated over the allowable five-year period.

Replacement Value

A second method for examining tangible assets is to consider the cost of replacing all equipment and supplies. The replacement value would not typically be the value assigned to used equipment, but the current cost of replacement can serve as an important benchmark from which to calculate the remaining useful life or the market value of individual items.

The replacement value for each item of inventory can be determined by engaging sales consultants who specialize in medical and office equipment, or by researching current prices through sales literature. The literature might present list prices, which may require adjustments to determine the actual selling prices.

Remaining Useful Life Value

The current value of equipment can be described by estimating how long it can be expected to last until it needs to be replaced. The remaining useful life of each item of equipment may be estimated by examining the current condition of the equipment, comparing the current condition to that of a comparable item in new condition, and estimating how much "life" is left in economic terms. In essence, the technique yields an estimate of the depreciated value in terms of the item's actual usefulness rather than in terms of what the IRS allows. The process lends itself well to a spreadsheet, as demonstrated in Exhibit 2–1.

Estimating how much "life" is left in any particular piece of equipment may be the most difficult part of applying the technique. The appraiser can gain insight from the perspective of sales professionals by asking them how long they estimate the equipment will last. The answer may be biased in two ways, which could balance each other. If the salesperson is interested in convincing you that her equipment is durable and dependable, you may hear that the equipment will last a very long time. If the prospect of frequent purchases (and frequent commissions) sways her, you may hear that you should expect to replace the item every few years. A balancing tactic is to find out what the manufacturer's warranty implies about the durability of the product.

The usefulness of the equipment is also impacted by the extent it is used, and the volume and conditions under which it is used should impact the appraiser's opinion of value. An exam table that is seldom used may have a considerable amount of "life" left, even if it is 10 or 15 years old.

The remaining useful life of equipment is affected by technological advances. There have been extensive developments in office laboratory equipment in the past decade, thanks in part to advances in microprocessors. The original cost of certain items purchased just five years ago may not be a valid comparable replacement cost on which to estimate the remaining useful life. If technological improvements have rendered the item obsolete, its value may be negligible. On the other hand, technological obsolescence doesn't necessarily mean that an item of equipment is no

EXHIBIT 2-1

Remaining Useful Life of Equipment

Item	A Replacement Value (from catalog)	B Estimated Total Life (from salesperson)	C Current Age (from internal records)	D Estimated Remaining Life (B – C)	E Percent of Remaining Life (D / B)	F Estimated Remaining Value (A x E)

longer useful as a revenue-producing instrument. For example, a well-maintained and calibrated balance scale is still useful even though electronic scales may be more convenient or more consistently accurate.

Market Value

The true market value of a particular item of equipment may be higher or lower than the estimate of the remaining useful life might imply. The market value can only be determined, however, if there are competitive alternatives for the seller to dispose of the equipment. The market for used medical office equipment is not a particularly active one in most geographic regions of the country. Used office equipment is readily bought and sold, however, and clues to the value of these items can be obtained by securing an offer to purchase from a dealer in used office equipment. I have observed certain items of equipment that may actually have greater market value as antiques than their remaining useful life would imply.

The market value may also be impacted by the value that equipment may have if it is donated to a charitable organization. Medical missions organizations are constantly searching for medical office equipment that can be redeployed in an environment where the items are desperately needed in spite of their perceived obsolescence. The tax-deductible value of the donation may be a form of the market value that can serve as the basis for an appraisal.

RESTATING THE BALANCE SHEET

Why the Balance Sheet Is Insufficient

Determining the value of the tangible assets requires a restatement of the balance sheet for two important reasons. First, most medical practices are operated on the cash basis for tax purposes, but the accrual basis of accounting renders a more accurate picture of the current financial condition of the business for appraisal purposes. Second, generally accepted accounting principles don't require balance sheets to be constructed with all the components that are important to an understanding of the economic value of the business.

The cash basis of accounting recognizes revenue at the time it is collected, while the accrual basis recognizes it at the time it is earned. Therefore, a cash-basis balance sheet will not likely include accounts receivable, since the value of services they represent has not yet been collected. But to the owner of the practice, the accounts receivable can be converted to cash, so it is very important to recognize their value in the appraisal process. The value of accounts receivable is not likely to be equal to their face value. Discounts will need to be estimated based on the age and payer mix of the accounts, but the value is real, and recognizing that value requires a conversion to an economic balance sheet.

Constructing the Economic Balance Sheet

Balance sheets are constructed according to accounting standards to give a snapshot of the financial value of the business at a particular point in time. But the picture the balance sheet offers is only a partial view of the total value of the business. It may exclude particular components of value that are quite material to the seller, and it may include certain items that are of no value to the buyer. The appraisal should therefore include a restatement of the balance sheet to reflect the economic value or accrued value of the business rather than the cash value alone. Specific adjustments may be required in the following items:

Cash   The most recent balance sheet is
              likely to contain a cash balance that
              will differ from the cash on hand as of
              the date of the transaction. In many

cases, the sellers will be motivated to distribute all cash remaining at the close of business on the day prior to the transaction, which means the new owner will not likely be purchasing any cash from the seller.

Accounts Receivable
If they are currently excluded from the balance sheet, they will need to be included in the adjusted balance sheet (with an allowance for doubtful accounts), to obtain a more complete picture of the value of the tangible assets.

Prepaid Expenses
Items such as annual premiums for professional liability insurance may have remaining value, and should be included on the economic balance sheet even if they are excluded from the cash-basis balance sheet. If the insurance remains in force, its value is being purchased by the new owner. If the insurance is replaced, a refund can be expected, and its value should be recognized.

Fixed Assets
The cash-basis balance sheet will include fixed assets, with the IRS allowance for depreciation. An adjustment may be required to reflect the market value or the remaining useful life value, according to the purpose of the appraisal.

Goodwill
Goodwill is likely to be omitted from the current balance sheet unless the seller paid a previous owner an amount in excess of tangible assets that was booked as goodwill. The current value of goodwill, if any, will

Liabilities

need to come from an analysis of the techniques described in Chapter 3. The cash-basis balance sheet is likely to exclude transactions incurred but not yet paid for, such as accounts payable, accrued vacation, accrued payroll taxes, and unstated buyout-related notes to former stockholders. Liabilities that should be excluded from the economic balance sheet might include loans to stockholders, loans secured by personal vehicles, or other owner-related transactions.

Exhibit 2–2 offers an example of an adjusted balance sheet.

EXHIBIT 2-2

Balance Sheet Adjustments

	Current	Economic	
ASSETS			
Cash	$16,325	$0	
Accounts Receivable	$0	$152,948	
Less discount for uncollectibles	$0	($27,539)	based on analysis of age and payer mix
Net receivables	$0	$125,409	
Prepaid Expenses	$0	$12,306	
Fixed Assets	$53,191		
Less depreciation	($25,315)		
Net of depreciation	$27,876		
At market value	$0	$17,500	based on appraisal
Goodwill	$0	$150,000	based on appraisal
TOTAL ASSETS	$72,077	$430,624	
LIABILITIES			
Loan to owner	$10,000	$0	
Bank loan for Corvette	$16,523	$0	to be excluded from sale of practice
TOTAL LIABILITIES	$26,523	$0	
EQUITY	$45,554	$430,624	
TOTAL LIABILITIES AND EQUITY	$72,077	$430,624	

3

C H A P T E R

Traditional Methods for Measuring the Value of Intangibles (Goodwill)

How can you buy something you cannot hold? What independent value does a medical practice have when the revenue stream is intrinsically tied to the physicians' personal practice style? Few issues in deal making incite as much controversy as this one does. Sellers place an intuitive and personal value on goodwill, but buyers are reluctant to pay for it. The erratic dynamics of shifting healthcare markets sometimes result in irrational decisions about the emotion-filled value of goodwill, with outcomes that have long-term negative consequences for buyers and their communities.

Goodwill values in a medical practice are arguable. In fact, they have been the focus of contention in thousands of divorce cases involving professionals, and the conclusions reached have been widely varying. The intangible value of a medical practice is frequently so closely tied to the personal, nontransferrable skills and qualities of the individual practitioner as to make measuring goodwill value an assumption-filled exercise. With each assumption comes the potential for argument and an increase in the business risk of decisions made on the basis of goodwill value.

How can we manage those business risks? What should we know about the assumptions underlying goodwill values that can help us reach fair conclusions? These are some of the tough issues the next two chapters will attempt to address. In this chapter I will introduce three of the frequently applied methods for measuring goodwill in small businesses. I will describe the techniques and offer examples of how they might be used, and offer questions for their critique.

In Chapter 4, I want to introduce a series of approaches to measuring the value of goodwill that I think can restore rational decision making and fairness without damaging the foundations of healthcare delivery systems. The replacement method is based on the not-so-radical idea that buyers have a choice. They can develop a practice from scratch or they can buy an existing enterprise. And they will make their decision on the basis of which choice makes the most economic sense. The excess earnings approach acknowledges that the present value is based on the future value *that can actually accrue to the buyer.* The technique makes a clear distinction, perhaps for the first time, between the goodwill value that is transferrable and the goodwill value that is not transferrable.

Admittedly, the process of measuring business values is part science and part art. The professional judgment of the appraiser still plays a major role, but informed judgment is superior to uninformed emotion in terms of producing a win–win outcome. The techniques introduced in Chapters 3 and 4 won't reduce the reliance on professional judgment, but they are designed to contribute to a sharpening of that judgment in the hopes that buyers and sellers will make deals that preserve the community's interests.

DEFINING INTANGIBLES

First, let's review the definition of the intangible value of a medical practice.

There are several components to the intangible value of any business. The value of a business is dependent on all the factors that make it successful. That may include such things as the location, the attractiveness to clients, the accessibility to new business, the user-friendliness of the business, the systems that enable it to operate efficiently, the reasons why people keep coming back for more services, and the strength of reputation that builds loyalty and referrals.

The medical practice is dependent on all those factors, but may also be enriched by additional components of goodwill. The financial well-being of a medical practice is also enhanced by a payer mix that offers the business owners the stability of a diversified patient base combined with limited contractual discounts. Business success in managed care markets depends on developing systems for tracking referrals and the costs of managing the care of specific patient groups. Increasing the revenue stream in a medical group can come from maintaining a comprehensive product line that keeps referrals in-house as much as possible. In these components of intangible business value, the attention is on those factors that are *transferrable* to another owner. In Chapter 1 we described these as components of corporate goodwill.

It is important to recognize characteristics of goodwill that are less able to be transferred to another owner and to segregate such characteristics from the systems that render financial success. Nontransferrable goodwill might include the charismatic manner of an individual physician, extraordinary time-management ability, a high profile in the community, or a specific unique medical skill. The difficulty comes in discerning the difference between financial success that comes from corporate goodwill and that which comes from the personal goodwill of the physician. The techniques described in this chapter and the next are designed to be surrogate measurements for the goodwill of a medical practice that comes from establishing and maintaining excellent business systems.

TRADITIONAL METHODS FOR MEASURING GOODWILL

The appraisal disciplines have developed a variety of common techniques for measuring business values in a broad spectrum of industries. The techniques that form the core of the discipline have impressive names:

> Discounted cash flow analysis
> Capitalization of earnings
> Guideline comparison methods

Discounted Cash Flow Analysis

The discounted cash flow (DCF) analysis method is based on two key assumptions. First, it is based on the concept that a business's value is represented by its ability to generate cash flow. The more cash a business can generate, the more valuable is its goodwill. Cash flow is a mirror of goodwill. The second assumption is that future owners of the business are willing to take a measured risk to gain access to that cash flow. They have a certain expectation of gaining a return on their investment. They are willing to buy into that cash flow, anticipating a reward for their infusion of capital. The appraisal process using the discounted cash flow analysis technique requires us to estimate both the cash flow and the required rate of return.

Estimating Cash Flow Estimating cash flow is the easier of these two assignments, although both processes require extensive judgment. Estimating cash flow requires forecasting the future benefits of cash flows to the business—typically for the next three to five years—after analyzing the factors that have led to success in the past, considering the ability of the practice's leadership to be competitive in the future, and estimating the impact of changes in the healthcare economy. A simple straight-line projection of historical cash flows will probably miss the mark unless the projection is qualified by other dynamics impacting the future of the business. Beyond three to five years, a terminal value is mathematically determined to complete the projection of future benefits.

Estimating the Discount Rate The discount rate is the denominator that represents the expected rate of return a buyer might make for an investment with similar risk. The future cash flows are divided by the discount rate to yield an estimate of net present value. Calculating an appropriate discount rate requires research. The discount rate is usually composed of three parts: It is the sum of a risk-free rate such as the current rate of return on a long-term Treasury note, plus a premium for the risks associated with the medical practice industry, plus another premium for the risks of the specific business.

A discount rate is the rate of return used to convert into present value a revenue stream or series of future revenue streams that are payable or receivable in the future. It is distinguished from a capitalization rate, which is an estimate of investment attractiveness. Capitalization rates are covered in the next section. Both rates are useful in deriving business valuation conclusions from analyzing revenue streams. *Understanding how and when to use discount rates and capitalization rates, and how to select those rates, is likely the most difficult problem appraisers face.* An excellent explanation of these two rates is given in *Valuing Small Businesses and Professional Practices* by Shannon Pratt.

Finding the risk-free rate is usually as simple as looking up the current return for a 10-year Treasury note in the latest *Wall Street Journal.* It is considered a "risk-free" rate simply because it is the rate of return an investor can expect without taking the risks associated with an open market. U.S. Treasury notes are backed by the United States government, and are considered among the safest investments an individual can make.

Estimating the industry-specific risk premium is less intuitive. While the typical appraiser seems to establish the medical industry risk premium at between 2 and 4 percentage points, this pattern seems to have evolved more from practice than from any documented risk history. There is limited public data to monitor. The recent emergence of investor-owned medical practices may eventually offer a glimpse into the risks of operating a medical practice as perceived by the investing public, but specific risk-defining data on privately held practices is virtually nonexistent. Moreover, the dynamics of the healthcare market are changing so rapidly—and in some cases, so violently—as to make projections of future risk in the industry all the more speculative.

Evaluating the risk associated with the specific medical practice requires the highest professional judgment. I recommend comparing the practice to its peers in at least six to eight key measurements to determine its relative business risk. The measurements to consider may be drawn from the following list:

Average age of accounts receivable

Gross collection ratio (receipts / charges)

Net collection ratio (receipts / (charges–discounts))

Production per physician in relative value units

Production per physician in gross charges

Production per physician in net receipts

Overhead ratio as a percent of net receipts

Full-time equivalent (FTE) staff per FTE physician

Active medical records per physician

Average fee per relative value unit

Comparisons to peer practices can be made on these measurements using data from the American Medical Association, the Medical Group Management Association, or *Medical Economics*. Practices that demonstrate a performance that is consistently better than that of their peers might be considered more highly rewarded, and therefore greater risk takers, than the average among physicians in their specialty. Worse-than-average performance would result in a lower premium.

The steps in performing a discounted cash flow analysis are as follows:

1. Project future earnings that will accrue to the benefit of the new owners, year by year, for three to five years.

2. Select a discount rate sufficient to attract capital, taking the issues listed above into consideration.

3. Determine the present value of each future year's earnings by dividing the projected earnings by the discount rate. (Tables of discount rates are presented in Appendix C.)

4. Total the net present values of the future years' earnings.

5. Estimate the residual value of the medical practice at the end of the projection period, discount it to the present period, and add the calculation to the total derived in step 4. This new total is the final figure for the total net present value of the medical practice.

Exibit 3–1 offers an example of how the discounted cash flow method can be used to produce an estimate of value.

Capitalization of Earnings

The capitalization of earnings method is simpler in some respects than the discounted cash flow analysis. It is simpler because it is usually applied to a single number representing income, such as normalized annual earnings, rather than a series of numbers. It is also simpler because it is usually applied to historical data rather than to projected revenue streams. A capitalization rate is any divisor (usually expressed as a percentage) that is used to convert income into value.

Some of the steps involved in developing a business valuation based on the capitalization of earnings sound quite similar to the steps involved in applying the discounted cash flow method.

The capitalization of earnings method involves two variables. The appraiser must determine what earnings to examine and what capitalization rate to apply to those earnings.

EXHIBIT 3-1

Example of Discounted Cash Flow Analysis

Step 1. The following projections of excess physician compensation (earnings above the median for the specialty) are made for a family practice group of four physicians:

Excess Compensation

Year 1	$40,000
Year 2	$60,000
Year 3	$100,000
Year 4	$140,000
Year 5	$200,000

Step 2. The discount rate is built up to yield the following conclusion:

Risk-free rate	7.0%
Industry-specific rate	4.0%
Practice-specific rate	12.0%
Total	23.0%

Step 3. Each year's projected cash flow is discounted to the present value. (The discount rates are presented in Appendix C.) The result of applying the formula yields the following calculations:

	Compensation	Divided by Discount Rate	Net Present Value
Year 1	$40,000	1.23	$32,520
Year 2	$60,000	1.51	$39,735
Year 3	$100,000	1.86	$53,763
Year 4	$140,000	2.29	$61,135
Year 5	$200,000	2.82	$70,922

Step 4. Add the net present values for each year.

Year 1	$32,520
Year 2	$39,735
Year 3	$53,763
Year 4	$61,135
Year 5	$70,922
Subtotal	$258,075

Step 5. Estimate the residual value at the end of the period, discount it, and add the discounted value to the total of Step 4. For the purposes of this example, we will assume the residual value to be limited to the tangible assets at the end of five years, with a projected value of $100,000.

The net present value of $100,000 at five years, discounted at 23 percent, equals $35,520. This added to the subtotal of Step 4 yields:

NPV of five years	$258,075
Residual value	$35,520
Final value	$293,595
Rounded	$290,000

Determining Applicable Earnings   The capitalization of earnings technique can be applied to historical, current, or expected future earnings. Historical data on physician earnings may be the most accessible and accurate of the three types, but it may not be the most appropriate measure of future earnings. As managed care alters the landscape, physicians' earnings in some specialties have begun to dip, and they are not expected to recover anytime soon. Assessing so-called "normalized earnings" is the appraiser's typical answer to the dilemma. Developing an estimate of normalized earnings involves analyzing the pattern of historical earnings and tempering conclusions about what might be "normal" in the future based on what is known about competitive forces impacting the specialty and the practice. Judgment plays a large role in developing normalized earnings, as in other parts of the appraisal process.

Capitalization Rates   Appraisers can usually find market information from which to infer capitalization rates (or cap rates, as they are called in our nickname culture) in every industry *except the medical practices industry*. Price-earnings multiples of publicly traded stocks give clues about the investor's expectations. When a stock sells at low price-earnings multiples of say, five times earnings, investors are telling the market that they consider the investment risky enough to demand a 20 percent return on their investment. A hot-selling stock priced at 40 times its annual earnings is attracting buyers who expect no more than a 2.5 percent return on their investment, based on the historical dividend stream. Buyers attracted at these prices may hope for higher total returns based on rising stock prices, but they are taking greater risks.

But public ownership of medical practices is still such a small segment of the market that using the price-earnings multiples of companies like PhyCor and Pacific Physician Services as clues to market-based capitalization rates would be inappropriate. What we are left with at this point is to build up a cap rate as we did with the discount rate. Cap rates can be derived by examining the safe rate of a T-bill yield, then adding premiums for industry-specific risk and the individual business risk.

The steps in performing the capitalization of earnings technique are as follows:

1. Estimate normalized earnings that have accrued to the benefit of the physicians for the past three to five years. Temper the estimate with known factors that can be projected to have a significant impact on the future income stream.
2. Select a discount rate sufficient to attract capital, taking the issues listed above into consideration.
3. Determine the business value of the medical practice by dividing the normalized earnings by the capitalization rate. The mathematical formula is:

$$\frac{\text{normalized earnings}}{\text{capitalization rate}} = \text{value}$$

The capitalization technique is demonstrated in Exibit 3–2.

Guideline Comparison Method

The third traditional method we will explore is appealing in its simplicity and in its affirmation of our intuition. The guideline comparison method is based on the idea that business value is based on what the market will bear, regardless of an analysis of income streams. The market has the ultimate say over what any given property is worth. If we can only compare the seller's property to that of other recent documented transactions, we will be able to determine the fair market value as only the market can determine.

The method is appealing and it is valid in many circumstances, but its validity and utility are limited to the availability of data on documented transactions of similar medical practices. Comparing the value of a medical practice to the value of a flower shop or any other small business is ludicrous, even if data on flower shop transactions is widely available.

EXHIBIT 3-2

Example of Capitalization Rate Technique

Step 1. Determine normalized earnings.

Let's assume the following pattern of earnings for a solo physician in OB/GYN for the past four years:

Year 1	$170,000
Year 2	$180,000
Year 3	$180,000
Year 4	$180,000

The pattern in this case seems quite predictable and normalized without adjustment, so we may conclude that her normalized earnings are $180,000.

Step 2. The capitalization rate is built up to yield the following conclusion:

Risk-free rate	7.0%
Industry-specific rate	5.0%
Practice-specific rate	18.0%
Total	30.0%

Step 3. Divide the normalized earnings by the capitalization rate to yield a business value.

$$\frac{\$180,000}{30\%} = \$600,000$$

Data on medical practice acquisitions has been limited to three main sources. The longest-running database is maintained by The Health Care Group of Plymouth Meeting, Pennsylvania. Their *Goodwill Registry* has tracked medical practice sales transactions since 1985, and the annual update now contains comparative data on over 2,000 acquisitions. The data is gleaned from reports volunteered by consultants around the country, and includes data on transactions involving most specialties and states. The Institute of Business Appraisers in Boynton Beach, Florida, offers a smaller database with slightly more detail to its members. A recent publication entitled *The 1995 Practice Acquisition Resource Book,* produced by the Center for Healthcare Industry Performance Studies of Columbus, Ohio, details data on hospital acquisitions of medical practices. Other consulting organizations—including Hekman & Associates, Inc.—maintain private databases of comparable transactions within their experience.

The most common point of comparison in most databases is the ratio of the price to the annual gross revenues. The multiple of earnings is a simple benchmark, easily calculated and understood. Its simplicity is deceptively appealing. The conclusions of value have been based on a multiplicity of methods, as well as on appraisal techniques applied with enormous variation in skill. The result of these applications and misapplications of appraisal techniques has been wildly variant. The *1995 Goodwill Registry* reports, for example, that over the past few years, family practice acquisitions have transpired with goodwill values anywhere from zero to 250 percent of net receipts. The lack of standard definitions, combined with the reliance on voluntary submissions of information, make the databases by themselves of limited value in determining the fair market value of a medical practice. They may play a role in affirming the ballpark value of a practice, or in checking the reality of other methods, but basing a major transaction on the national market data alone is similar to buying a car on the basis of the dealer's sticker price.

Troubling Traditions

These three methods (discounted cash flow analysis, capitalization of earnings, and guideline comparison) and dozens of their derivatives have emerged over the past few decades as the primary techniques for measuring goodwill value in small businesses. Their direct application to medical practice valuation, however, requires assumptions about similarities to other small businesses that are more difficult to accept. Some of these assumptions are as follows:

1. *Any investor can acquire any business, which means that a prudent investor will decide which acquisition among several industries is most sound on the basis of financial and marketing evidence.*

The reality in medical practices is that they are not (yet) widely investor-owned enterprises. The owners of medical practices have historically been almost exclusively physicians, a limited part of the total investing population that maintains its exclusivity by rigorous professional licensing. Medical practices are bought and sold in closed markets rather than open markets.

2. *Buyers of businesses are focused mostly on the return on investment and the lifestyle they will attain by taking the risks of business ownership.*

Buyers of medical practices are not just buying a job for themselves. In the case of many hospitals that actively acquire medical practices, the buyers' intent has nothing to do with a direct return on investment or lifestyle. It has to do with gaining a strategic advantage within a complex and dynamic healthcare industry.

3. *Conclusions about business value can be derived by comparing the specifics of the targeted business with widely used data from a broad spectrum of same-industry businesses.*

Comparative data in the medical practice acquisition world is extremely limited in both volume and utility. The databases that are in existence are based on voluntary submission of information, without standardization of definitions, and contain insufficient volume in any specific market to yield statistically valid conclusions.

These assumptions, despite their weaknesses in adapting to the healthcare world, are the foundation for traditional appraisal services.

These methods each have derivatives that refine the definitions even further. Some appraisal practitioners focus on net cash flow before taxes; others give their attention to net profits after taxes. Still others insist that the capitalization rates must be derived in a four-step buildup process, while others look to market trends within appraisal disciplines to document their choice for capitalization rates.

The dilemma we face in healthcare is that mergers and acquisitions are required for physicians and hospitals to remain relevant to their communities, but we don't have very good tools for measuring business value and for constructing relevant organizations. Our understanding of valuation processes needs to take a giant step forward to catch up with the demands of a dynamic marketplace.

It is my hope that the valuation techniques described in the next chapter will at least represent a small step forward in the quest for the right tools. They are designed to build on the appraisal traditions developed in other industries, and to adapt those traditions to the world of healthcare.

4

New Traditions in Goodwill Measurement

In December 1995, *American Medical News* reported that "only 17 percent of institutions have posted positive returns on their practice investments."[1] The report goes on to cite the findings of a study of 5,300 hospital financial officers conducted by *Healthcare Financial Management* and by Physician Services of America of Louisville, Kentucky. Only 32 percent of respondents said that acquired physician practices have met revenue and expense projections set by the hospital.

We can speculate about what hospitals expected with their acquisitions and about how physicians responded when they no longer shouldered the business risk of a medical practice. In some cases, I'm sure both the buyer and seller were surprised to find that they weren't on the same wavelength in understanding what to do with the new relationship. My experience tells me that inadequate or nonexistent appraisals, and valuations based on the traditional

---

1. "Practices Sell, Hospitals Lose," *American Medical News,* December 11, 1995.

appraisal approaches, miss the mark when it comes to valuing a medical practice. Projecting revenue streams in an unstable industry requires great faith and intuition. Developing discount rates and capitalization rates in the absence of comparative data takes a large measure of professional judgment. Maybe too much judgment. The result is a growing segment of losing acquisitions. The long-term consequences of those losing ventures can only be a matter of speculation at this point, but even the casual observer of the healthcare market can sense that the losses cannot continue.

To a partial extent, the losing traditions can be traced to inadequate or misapplied appraisal methods. The assumptions required to apply traditional techniques to the unique characteristics of medical practices simply don't fit. New models are required. It is time to introduce appraisal techniques for medical practices that fit the environment and contribute to rational deal making.

ALTERNATIVE METHODS FOR MEASURING GOODWILL

As you can see, measuring the business value of a medical practice with traditional methods can get tedious and irrelevant in a hurry. The traditional methods seem to call for a stretch of imagination. Developing meaningful capitalization rates, for example, requires us to trust the appraiser's judgment where there is no data to support his conclusions. Even comparing goodwill values to national data registries, while appealing in its simplicity, misses the point about finding the essential value of a local medical group with local competition.

Perhaps the most awkward aspect of all in valuing medical practices is that the most common buyer, the hospital, isn't interested in earning a direct return on the investment at all. The real value of owning practices is in realizing a steady stream of business for the hospital and its ancillary services, and in becoming a sizable negotiating force with healthcare buyers. But measuring those values borders on the illegal. Imagine what might happen if a hospital based its bid for a medical practice on documentation of the new revenue associated with switched referral patterns. The FTC and the IRS would likely be knocking on the door within days. Cries of private inurement and unfair competition would be on the lips of every competing hospital within a hundred miles.

Even in mergers of two or more practices, the traditional appraisal methods seem to miss the point. The future benefit isn't in the revenue stream of the acquired practice. It's not even in the opportunity to gain economies of scale and the associated cost reductions. History shows that most larger groups aren't necessarily more cost-effective. The real benefit is in the stronger negotiating position the merged group enjoys. The value of that future benefit lies in the hope that being bigger will translate to getting better deals in the managed care market and that the new group will gain momentum to attract more physicians and more capital. These future benefits are what brings potential merger partners to the table, but such benefits are not measured by any of the traditional appraisal methods.

The fact is that if any organization wants to grow and to extend its market share and its influence, it needs to increase its capacity to meet the needs of its market. And there are just two ways to do that: make or buy. A hospital that wants to improve its position can employ physicians and set them up in practice, or it can acquire existing practices. Medical groups that want to become larger can recruit new physicians and support them until they reach a break-even point, or they can acquire well-established practices in their market.

Another complication in determining the fair market value of a medical practice is the interrelated decision about how to compensate physicians after the transaction. In my experience, most physicians expect their compensation to remain the same, or increase, after the transaction, even though they will no longer bear the bulk of the business risk. Most hospitals seem to have accepted these conditions through a combination of naive expectations, off-balance-sheet calculations, or perceived market pressures. Paying physician salaries and overhead costs in excess of direct professional fees frequently finds justification in factors that none of the traditional appraisal methods take into consideration. The excess earnings amount to a premium for the acquisition.

These stark dilemmas call for alternative techniques for measuring the value of a medical practice—techniques that reflect market realities more than mathematical gymnastics. I would propose two methods that stand apart as rational approaches to restoring sound business decisions in a chaotic and frenetic market.

The two methods that seem to me to be most helpful are a unique derivative of the replacement method, and an excess earnings method used in conjunction with tangible assets. The tangible assets component of this method requires the construction of an economic balance sheet, as was described in Chapter 2.

Replacement Method

One of the most helpful ways of establishing the value of a medical practice is to estimate the cost of replicating it. A surrogate measure for gauging the business risk associated with a practice is to look at the potential cost of starting that business over again. The replacement method of appraisal introduces a sobering dose of reality for both buyers and sellers. It becomes abundantly clear that there are real options to completing the transaction. The fair market value of a particular medical practice emerges more clearly when the buyer considers the valid competitive alternative of starting a new practice from scratch.

The replacement method is also among the simplest of techniques to apply, and the combination of its market realism and elementary mathematics makes it a powerful technique in almost any situation. The task of estimating the cost of replacement can be accomplished by most physicians with computer skills, a curious mind, and a penchant for research. Executives skilled in developing operating and capital budgets can put a basic pro forma together, and research the practicalities of medical business start-ups, by talking with experienced physicians.

The following steps will be required in applying the replacement method:

1. Prepare an operating budget for three years, or until the practice is projected to reach a normalized, mature income stream. The timing of the break-even point might be estimated on the basis of the competitive environment for the specialty and on the historical growth patterns of recent arrivals to the medical community. Be sure to include the financing costs of capital items such as medical and office equipment, leasehold improvements, accounts receivable, and working capital.

2. Estimate the one-time costs related to physician recruitment, including the administrative time and hospitality expenses for hosting multiple candidates.

3. Total the costs derived from the first two steps.

The result of a systematic projection of costs associated with a start-up will serve as an important benchmark in the negotiation process.

I am familiar with several situations in which hospitals grossly underestimated the cost of starting up their own practices, and failed to cut their losses when they became apparent. The long-term losses in these situations have amounted to millions of dollars, even for small practices. The lesson of these situations is to be realistic in the projections, and to be astute when the projections turn out to be unrealistic. Exhibit 4–1 demonstrates a simple example of the replacement method.

An example of a fully developed appraisal applying the replacement method is found in the Boondocks Family Health Center case study at the end of this chapter.

EXHIBIT 4-1

Replacement Method

Step 1.	Prepare a three year operating budget.			
		Year 1	**Year 2**	**Year 3**
	Revenues	$120,000	$280,000	$330,000
	Expenses	$250,000	$260,000	$300,000
	Profit (Loss)	($130,000)	$20,000	$30,000
	Net three-year loss = ($80,000)			
Step 2.	Estimate the one-time costs of recruitment.			
	Hosting six candidates @ $1,000 each	$6,000		
	Administrative time	$5,000		
	Recruiter's fee	$20,000		
	Legal fees for contracting	$3,000		
	Total one-time costs	$34,000		
Step 3.	Total the sunk costs (Step 1 + Step 2).			
	Operating losses	$80,000		
	Recruitment costs	$34,000		
	Total	$114,000		

Excess Earnings Plus Tangible Assets

The excess earnings method calls for an analysis of the historical earnings patterns, and it specifically measures the portion that is above average for the specialty. The theory behind the excess earnings method is that only the portion of a physician's income that is above average is attributable to goodwill. Every physician is assumed to be capable of earning a median income within his specialty, but only those who have developed ways to leverage their potential earn rewards in the form of above-average earnings.

While measuring excess earnings may be systematic, interpreting the value of the business on their basis alone is not. Above-average earnings may indeed be an indicator of goodwill, but the appraiser still must discern whether the reward was earned because of corporate goodwill, which is transferrable to another owner, or personal goodwill, which is not transferrable. Likewise, the buyer, who wants to pay only for the future benefits of ownership of the business, will need to segregate the portion of the future excess earnings she hopes to retain from the portion she may want to keep in the business as an incentive for the continued service of existing physicians in the practice.

Applying the excess earnings method requires research both within the practice and outside it.

1. The income statements of the past five years must be assembled and adjusted to yield economic income statements, as outlined in Chapter 2. The goal of these adjustments is to derive a complete picture of owners' discretionary income, including benefits typically reserved for owners of closely held businesses.

2. Data on median incomes for the specialty will need to be assembled for the same period of time from national sources such as the American Medical Association, the Medical Group Management Association, or *Medical Economics*.

3. Using a spreadsheet, calculate the difference between the actual physician compensation and the median compensation within the specialty for each year in the study.

4. Identify the potential new net revenue that can be realistically projected to be generated in the next five years based on anticipated business developments. These may include improvements in operating efficiency, fee schedule adjustments, extended hours of availability, or other strategic or management initiatives.

5. Add the historical excess earnings of the past five years to the projected net new revenue for the next five years. Subtract the portion of excess earnings anticipated to be retained in the business for incentive compensation. The remainder is the total future value of goodwill available to the new owner for the next five years.

6. The goodwill value is then added to the net assets derived from the construction of an economic

balance sheet, as described in Chapter 2, to yield a total value of the business. Exhibit 4–2 demonstrates an example of the application of this technique.

This method might be considered unconventional in the eyes of the appraisal disciplines. It combines historical earnings data with projections of unlike data, and includes no terminal value for the income stream beyond five years. My rationale for structuring the formula this way is based on the following observations:

a. The five-year time period for reviewing the historical pattern and the future projections is based on the typical financing expectation. Most commercial loans for small businesses are established with five-year paybacks. In any case, the periods need to be matched. The focus is on developing a rational revenue stream that benefits the new owner, segregated from the physicians who continue to practice in the business.

b. Five years is a long time in the current healthcare environment. Offering a terminal value at any arbitrary point implies that the business will be as we know it in perpetuity, an assumption that many in the healthcare industry will readily challenge. In medical practices in particular, a 20 percent annual turnover of patients is common, and turnover rates may increase as managed care contracts shift market shares.

c. The major improvement in this method over more conventional approaches is that it measures only the goodwill value that is reasonably transferrable. This portion of goodwill, combined with the economic value of tangible assets, offers a value that can earn a realistic return on investment. It also articulates the source of future net revenues by requiring a disciplined approach to business planning.

EXHIBIT 4–2

Excess Earnings Plus Tangible Assets

Step 1. The income statements of the past five years must be assembled and adjusted to yield economic income statements, as outlined in Chapter 2. The goal of these adjustments is to derive a complete picture of owners' compensation, including benefits typically reserved for owners of closely held businesses.

Year	W-2 Income	Adjustments	Actual Income
1991	$200,000	$27,254	$227,254
1992	$210,000	$39,963	$249,963
1993	$180,000	$68,414	$248,414
1994	$200,000	$36,972	$236,972
1995	$250,000	$47,329	$297,329

Step 2. Data on median incomes for the specialty will need to be assembled for the same period of time from national sources such as the American Medical Association, the Medical Group Management Association, or *Medical Economics.*

Year	Mean for the Specialty (AMA data)
1991	$111,500
1992	$114,400
1993	$116,800
1994	$120,000
1995	$125,000

Step 3. Using a spreadsheet, calculate the difference between the actual physician compensation and the median compensation within the specialty for each year in the study.

Net Income	AMA Mean	Actual Dr. Y	Excess Dr. Y
1991	$111,500	$227,254	$115,754
1992	$114,400	$249,963	$135,563
1993	$116,800	$248,414	$131,614
1994	$120,000	$236,972	$116,972
1995	$125,000	$297,329	$172,329
Total			$672,232

(continued)

EXHIBIT 4-2 —*Concluded*

Excess Earnings Plus Tangible Assets

Step 4. Identify the potential new net revenue that can be realistically projected to be generated in the next five years based on anticipated business developments. These may include improvements in operating efficiency, fee schedule adjustments, extended hours of availability, or other strategic or management initiatives.

Initiative	Revenue	Cost	Net Revenue
Computerization	$0	$30,000	($30,000)
Fee schedule enhancements	$100,000	$0	$100,000
Extended hours	$300,000	$250,000	$50,000
Total			$120,000

Step 5. Add the historical excess earnings of the past five years to the projected net new revenue for the next five years. Subtract the portion of excess earnings anticipated to be retained in the business for incentive compensation. The remainder is the total future value of goodwill available to the new owner for the next five years.

Historical excess earnings (rounded)	$672,000
Projected net new revenue	$120,000
Retained for incentives	($700,000)
Remaining net goodwill	$92,000

Step 6. The goodwill value is then added to the net assets derived from the construction of an economic balance sheet, as described in Chapter 2, to yield a total value of the business.

Remaining net goodwill	$92,000
Economic balance sheet equity (hypothetical)	$100,000
Total appraised value	$192,000

REALITY CHECKS

In theory, rational approaches should yield rational results. But in the practice of appraising medical practices, it is wise to apply some reality checks to the end result, just to make sure the theory and the practice fit.

Every buyer of a medical practice should answer this "do-or-die" question: Exactly when and how will our investment break even? If the answer is unclear, go back to the appraisal process. If it is unacceptable, go back to the negotiating table.

Before an appraised value is accepted, both the buyer
and the seller should thoroughly think through the implications of the proposed deal. The issues highlighted in Chapter 10 are worthy of review when the appraisal is done. Let
the dynamics of life after the deal shape your perception of
value and serve as another series of reality checks. The appraiser can render independent perspectives, but the parties that have to live with the deal are the ones that have to
accept, reject, or modify those perspectives.

ADJUSTMENTS AND WEIGHTING

All the appraisal techniques that fit a given situation
should be applied in order to offer more than one figure for
the potential value of the medical practice. The appraiser
then has two more opportunities to apply professional
judgment. The results of the multiple methods can be adjusted and weighted according to a variety of circumstances. Adjustments might be necessary to account for
such nuances as these:

- The minority shareholder position in a professional corporation. The share of the total business value held by a minority shareholder can be
  reasonably discounted, since the liquidity of his
  shares depends on the consensus of a majority of
  the shareholders.
- Recent developments in the market or in the
  business that impact the business value. The an-
  nouncement of a new surgicenter planned for adjacent property, for example, might enhance the
  value of an ophthalmology practice, unless the
  new center is owned by a competitor.
- The economic decline of the surrounding community can devalue a medical practice if rising un-
  employment translates to lower collection ratios.

The appraiser may also select a value that is composed of multiple approaches with unequal weights. The

importance attached to specific methods might depend on the appraiser's perception of the validity of the data, the appropriateness of the method, or the result of reality checks.

CONCLUSION

Measuring the value of a business requires a blend of techniques and perspectives. There are many right answers to the question of the value of any particular business, but the best answers are those that focus on the measurement of future benefits to the new owners of the business. The nontraditional techniques introduced in this chapter offer some industry-insider alternatives designed to achieve some of the better answers.

Boondocks Family Health Center Practice Appraisal

Description of the Assignment

Boondocks Family Health Center requested an independent appraisal of the tangible and intangible assets of the group medical practice, in anticipation of discussions with potential buyers. Two potential buyers have expressed specific interest in the group, and the physicians are examining all their options for optimizing their business potential either by remaining independent and increasing the value of the practice, or by integrating with a strategically advantageous partner.

The standard of value to be used in this appraisal is the fair market value of the tangible and intangible assets, exclusive of real estate, as of February 23, 1996. Fair market value is defined in Revenue Ruling 59-60 as:

> . . . the price at which the property would change hands between a willing buyer and a willing seller when the former is not under any compulsion to act and the latter is not under any compulsion to sell, both parties having reasonable knowledge of relevant facts.

Description of the Property

The scope of this appraisal is to measure the fair market value of the tangible assets of cash, accounts receivable and equipment, and the intangible assets of the employees, the patient relationships, and the value of the practice as an ongoing concern. The appraisal officially excludes the value of the real estate portion of the assets, even though they are held in the professional corporation and appear on the balance sheet. The reason real estate is excluded is that the business valuation appraiser is not qualified to comment on the current value of local commercial property in the Boondocks region. The real estate value will be included by reference, however, to an appraisal conducted in November 1993. The total value of all assets includes the current valuation derived by this analysis and the unverified value of real estate as of November 1993. The appraisal of the office concluded in November 1993 that the value of the property at that time was $600,000, including a residential rental building that was acquired adjacent to the office in November 1992 for $74,500. The total remaining debt is approximately $270,000 on the two properties, rendering a net value, if the 1993 appraisal were still valid, of $330,000.

Limiting Conditions

The data gathered for the analysis of value were drawn from the financial statements, billing records, medical records, and from personal observations of the appraiser at the time of the site visit on February 22 and 23, 1996. Indications of the future stability of the practice were drawn from interviews with each of the five physicians.

Appraisal Approach

The value of the tangible and intangible assets of Boondocks Family Health Center can be inferred from an examination of financial and production data, using three main approaches. First, we will describe the net asset value of the tangible assets, then look at the replacement value of the practice, and finally conclude with consideration of the future value of excess earnings.

Appraiser's Disinterest

The appraiser hereby declares that he has no present or contemplated future interest in the subject property or any other interest that might tend to prevent his making a fair and unbiased appraisal.

VALUATION CONCLUSIONS

Net Asset Value

The first method calls for a restatement of book value after an examination of the collectible value of the accounts receivable, an appraisal of the equipment on the basis of its remaining useful life, and after adjustments, if any, for personal transactions. The net asset value measures the value of tangible assets only, and will be combined with the excess earnings method to yield a complete conclusion of total value.

The book value of the practice on December 31, 1995, was as follows:

Balance Sheet
BOONDOCKS FAMILY HEALTH CENTER
December 31, 1995

Assets

Cash and other current assets	$23,989		
Land	51,956		
Buildings	475,777		
Less depreciation	(104,218.)		
Furniture, Fixtures and Equipment	400,122		
Less Depreciation	(385,671.)		
TOTAL ASSETS			$461,956

Liabilities

Current liabilities	$5,428		
Notes payable	134,149		
TOTAL LIABILITIES		$341,962	

Equity

Capital stock	140,989		
Treasury stock	(16,832.)		
Retained earnings	12,762		
Net income (loss)	(16,926.)		
TOTAL EQUITY		119,994	
Total Liabilities and Equity			$461,956

The balance sheet is prepared according to generally accepted accounting principles, on the cash basis, by EPC, Certified Public Accountants. While it meets the standards for the Internal Revenue Service for bookkeeping functions, it does not include the fair market value of accounts receivable or the fair market value of the building, land, furniture, fixtures, and equipment. The balance sheet therefore needs to be restated with consideration for these assets at fair market value.

Accounts receivables are charges owned by patients and their insurers to Boondocks Family Health Center, P.C. They are booked at the standard fees, regardless of how they will be paid by the insurer. Medicare, Medicaid, HMOs, and other insurers frequently disallow a portion of the charge, resulting in a write-off of the uncollectible portion. In 1995, the company was able to recognize as income about 74 percent of its gross charges before contractual write-offs, and 95 percent of its gross charges after contractual write-offs. Income was recognized on the cash basis. Our objective with this part of the appraisal is to estimate the collectible value of the accounts receivable.

The accounts receivables have been relatively steady in the past year, but a computer conversion at the Medicaid carrier has caused significant delays in cash receipts, and escalated the accounts receivables. Based on the most recent statement (February 12, 1996), the accounts receivables can be valued to yield the following projections of cash:

Age	Book Value	Collectibility	Estimated Cash Value
0–30 days	$175,318	70%	$122,723
30–60 days	$76,709	65%	$49,861
60–90 days	$20,398	60%	$12,239
90–120 days	$7,508	40%	$3,003
120 days +	$67,069	20%	$13,414
Total	$347,002	58%	$201,240

The fair market value of furniture, fixtures, and equipment was determined by inspecting each item and judging its remaining useful life. The appraiser physically examined each piece of furniture, fixtures, and equipment, and determined that, in the aggregate, the remaining useful life is approximately 50 percent of the book value before depreciation. The bulk of the medical office furniture and equipment is approximately seven years old, and has been maintained in excellent condition. Applying the estimate yields the following conclusion of the value of furniture, fixtures, and equipment:

$$\$400,122 \times 50\% = \$200,000 \text{ (rounded)}$$

The value of the land and buildings is specifically excluded from this appraisal, so the restatement of the balance excludes the book value and the associated liabilities.

We are now ready for a restatement of the balance sheet as follows:

Restated Balance Sheet
BOONDOCKS FAMILY HEALTH CENTER
December 31, 1995

Assets

Cash and other current assets	$23,989	
Accounts receivables at FMV	201,240	
Furniture, Fixtures, and Equipment at FMV	200,000	
TOTAL ASSETS		$425,229
Liabilities		
Current liabilities	$5,428	
Notes payable	67,000	
TOTAL LIABILITIES		$72,428
Equity		
TOTAL EQUITY		352,801
Total Liabilities and Equity		$425,229

The key difference between the standard balance sheet and the restated balance sheet is the net equity. The restated equity, or economic value, as it may be referred to in appraisal disciplines, is approximately $232,000 greater than the book value, exclusive of the value of real estate. If the value of the real estate is $330,000 or better, as determined by the 1993 appraisal minus current property-secured debt, then the total net asset value is approximately $562,000.

Excess Earnings Plus Tangible Assets

Measuring historical excess earnings, and especially projecting them into the future, can offer insight to the intangible value of the practice, which can then be added to the tangible value to derive an understanding of the total value of the business. Excess earnings are defined as the portion of physician compensation earned that exceeds the median for the specialty in the time period considered. They are viewed as a surrogate measure of the factors of goodwill that allow the practice to generate stronger-than-usual revenue streams. When projected into the future, they can be predictors of the future benefit to the new owner who can exercise discretion over the excess revenue stream. A portion of that excess future revenue may be reinvested in the business or retained for incentive bonuses, but some of it may convert to new profits for the risk-takers. That portion, which ultimately is projected to benefit the new owners for the next five years, is the basis for the calculation of the present intangible value.

In the case of Boondocks Family Health Center, the past physician compensation patterns have not demonstrated excess earnings. The following table illustrates this point.

Average Physician Compensation, Boondocks Family Health Center, 1992–1995

	BFHC	MGMA
1992	$109,300	$112,600
1993	$108,400	$120,000
1994	$95,800	$122,000
1995	$97,400	$125,000 (est.)

Projecting physician compensation on the basis of historical patterns would clearly not show any value for goodwill on the basis of the excess earnings method. This would mean that the only value recognizable in the business would be the net asset value of tangible assets.

Our analysis of the future outlook for Boondocks Family Health Center is more optimistic than the historical patterns might demonstrate. The reason for the optimism is the state's planned initiative for a capitated Medicaid program that impacts 55 percent of the current patient base at the practice. The practice has demonstrated its ability to manage care for Medicaid patients efficiently. Our analysis of utilization data for Medicaid patients from November 1993 through August 1995 shows the Boondocks Family Health Center to be averaging costs at the thirtieth percentile statewide. In only 2 of the 22 months reviewed did the group have costs per enrollee worse than the median for the state. This means the group is consistently outperforming other primary care physicians in managing the care of their Medicaid patients. If this pattern continues and improves into the proposed capitation agreement, the group can expect to be rewarded handsomely for their performance, and are likely to see above-average earnings overall.

Measuring the extent and value of this excess with accuracy is impossible since the proposed contract has not yet been released. The only indicators of offerings thus far range from projections of $200 to $295 per member per month (PMPM). At $295, the state would be offering one of the richest Medicaid capitation rates in the nation, according to a study conducted for the National Institute for Health Care Management and published in its series titled *States As Payers: Managed Care for Medicaid Populations.* The study shows Arizona to have the highest rate, at $290 PMPM as of June 1994. Only seven states were above the national average of $156 PMPM.

The group's Medicaid utilization reports show the average cost per enrollee at the Boondocks Family Health Center to be approximately $21 per member per month below the statewide average, although the cost data appears incomplete. If this trend continues, regardless of the final capitation rates offered by the state, the group is likely to prosper. If the practice maintains the current estimated 3,500 Medicaid patients, and is allowed to retain just one-quarter of the risk margin, or $5 per member per month for the next year, the profit projections may be in the range of $200,000 above and beyond the current levels of revenue for Medicaid patients. If those projections prove accurate and stable for the next five years, the group could recognize an additional one million dollars in the projection period.

The net present value of the projected new Medicaid revenues, assuming a 3 percent rate of inflation, is approximately $916,000. If this value is added to the net asset value of tangible assets, estimated at $353,000, the total value with the excess earnings plus tangible assets method would be approximately $1,269,000.

Replacement Value

The theory behind the replacement value method is that the potential buyer has a choice of ways to enter the Boondocks market. The buyer could either buy the existing practice, or establish a competing one to displace it. The cost of displacement, or of replicating the existing practice, is a shadow of the value of the going concern, and can therefore serve as an inferred value of the present business.

The cost of replication may vary considerably, depending on the operational losses required to build the practice to a point of comparable profitability. The components of establishing a new practice, however, are fairly common. Based on the assumption that replicating the practice involves building it to the point of supporting five full-time family practitioners and one physicians assistant, the following three-year budget can be constructed:

Sample Budget for Five Family Practice Physicians

	Year 1	Year 2	Year 3
OPERATING REVENUE			
Gross Professional Fees	$750,000	$1,100,000	$1,500,000
less adjustments	($150,000)	($220,000)	($440,000)
Net after adjustments	$600,000	$880,000	$1,060,000
Capitation revenue	$50,000	$100,000	$200,000
Interest income '	$0	$0	$0
Miscellaneous income	$0	$0	$0
TOTAL OPERATING INCOME	$650,000	$980,000	$1,260,000
OPERATING EXPENSE			
Physician salaries	$500,000	$525,000	$550,000
Physician benefits	$60,000	$63,000	$66,000
Physician profit-sharing	$25,000	$26,250	$27,500
Physician-extender salaries	$35,000	$36,000	$37,000
Administrative and billing salaries	$120,000	$122,000	$124,000
Medical support salaries	$110,000	$112,000	$115,000
Reception salaries	$43,000	$44,000	$45,000
Nonphysician employee benefits	$20,000	$22,000	$24,000
Nonphysician employee profit-sharing	$15,000	$16,000	$17,000
Payroll taxes	$27,000	$28,000	$29,000
SUBTOTAL NONPHYSICIANS AND TAXES	$370,000	$380,000	$391,000
SUBTOTAL PHYSICIANS	$585,000	$614,250	$643,500
SUBTOTAL	$955,000	$994,250	$1,034,500
Physical Resources			
Ancillary service expense	$20,000	$21,000	$22,000
General medical supplies	$22,000	$23,000	$24,000
Office and housekeeping supplies	$7,000	$8,000	$9,000
Rent on Building	$68,000	$68,000	$68,000
Property insurance	$1,000	$1,000	$1,000
Utilities	$1,000	$1,000	$1,000
Rent on Furn., fixtures, equip.	$0	$0	$0
Depreciation	$45,000	$50,000	$50,000
SUBTOTAL	$164,000	$172,000	$175,000
Purchased Services			
Purchased medical and prof. serv.	$0	$0	$0
Data processing supplies	$5,000	$6,000	$7,000
Data processing equip. maint.	$6,000	$6,000	$6,000
Accounting and legal services	$6,000	$6,000	$6,000

(Continued)

Sample Budget for Five Family Practice Physicians—*Concluded*

	Year 1	Year 2	Year 3
Professional liability insurance	$55,000	$55,000	$55,000
Housekeeping, maint. and repairs	$6,000	$6,000	$6,000
SUBTOTAL	$78,000	$79,000	$80,000
General and Administrative Services			
Telephone and communications	$10,000	$11,000	$12,000
Promotion	$4,000	$4,000	$4,000
Postage	$10,000	$10,000	$11,000
Subscriptions	$100	$100	$100
Business travel and entertainment	$2,000	$2,000	$2,000
Business meals	$300	$300	$300
G & A—Employee related expenses	$1,000	$1,200	$1,200
Other G & A	$1,000	$1,000	$1,000
SUBTOTAL	$28,400	$29,600	$31,600
Interest and Taxes			
Interest expense	$10,000	$10,000	$10,000
Federal income tax	$0	$0	$0
Other tax	$0	$0	$0
SUBTOTAL	$10,000	$10,000	$10,000
Total Operating Expense	$1,235,400	$1,284,850	$1,331,100
Overhead Percent	100%	68%	55%
Net Profit (Loss)	($585,400)	($304,850)	($71,100)
Net Cash Flow	($540,400)	($254,850)	($21,100)
Capital Budget			
Furniture, Fixtures, and Equipment	$400,000	$0	$0
Physician recruitment	$150,000	$0	$0
Total	$550,000	$0	$0
Net Net Cash Flow	($1,090,400)	($254,850)	($21,100)
Accumulated Net Net Cash Flow	($1,090,400)	($1,345,250)	($1,366,350)

The projections show a loss of cash to a near-break-even point over three years of $1,366,350, which would be offset by an equity value of accounts receivable of between $200,000 and $250,000, which would be available upon liquidation. The net value of the existing practice, using the replacement method, can be concluded to be approximately $1,116,000.

Weighted Analysis

The two estimates of total value yield the following conclusions of value:

Excess Revenue Plus Tangible Assets	$1,269,000
Replacement Method	$1,116,000

A review of the assumptions leads the appraiser to conclude that each method is equal in its potential validity and invalidity, which brings us to give them equal weighting. The following conclusion of value can therefore be drawn as follows:

	Appraisal Value	Weight	Weighted Value
Excess Revenue Plus Tangible Assets	$1,269,000	50%	$634,500
Replacement Method	$1,116,000	50%	$558,000
Conclusion of Total Value			$1,192,500
Rounded			$1,200,000

Reality Check

As a final check of the feasibility of the valuation conclusion, it is helpful to compare the appraised value with the values demonstrated in other acquisitions of family practice groups. Two sources of data can be used for comparison. *The Goodwill Registry,* published annually by The Health Care Group of Plymouth Meeting, PA, shows that for the past 10 years of tracking goodwill values, family practice physicians have been able to attract an average of 30 percent of the previous year's earnings in goodwill value, with values ranging from zero percent to 250 percent of the previous year's earnings. At $916,000, the goodwill value using the excess earnings method is about 77 percent of 1995 earnings. The value appears high, but is potentially justified in light of the extensive breadth of procedural capabilities.

The second source of data is the just-released report of practice values entitled *The 1995 Physician Practice Acquisition Resource Book,* published by The Center for Healthcare Industry Performance Studies. The reference point for our review will exclude the value of real estate, bringing the appraised value of the business to $870,000 ($1,200,000–$330,000), or $174,000 per physician. The median value paid by hospitals for family practices over the past few years was just over $111,000 per physician, but just under $90,000 per physician in the southern states. Values for nonteaching practices were approximately $153,000 per physician, almost $50,000 more than for practices engaged in teaching.

Certification

I hereby certify that, to the best of my knowledge and belief, the statements of fact contained in this report are true and correct, and this report has been prepared in conformity with the Uniform Standards of Professional Appraisal Practice of The Appraisal Foundation and the Principles of Appraisal Practice and Code of Ethics of the American Society of Appraisers.

Appraisal Associates, Inc.

5
CHAPTER

Legal Land Mines

CAVEAT: This publication is designed to provide general information about the legal restrictions impacting medical practice acquisitions and mergers. However, this book cannot substitute for a comprehensive review of your particular circumstances by an experienced healthcare attorney. Because the law affecting healthcare providers continues to develop rapidly, providers should seek the advice of legal counsel with respect to their particular situation.

INTRODUCTION

If you are looking for legal restrictions that might prohibit a proposed transaction, you are likely to find them in this chapter. The laws governing mergers and acquisitions of medical practices have generally begun as adaptations of legal restrictions governing other segments of society. Antitrust laws, for example, have their roots in notorious turn-of-the-century business combinations that enabled large conglomerates to engage in price-fixing and other business activities contrary to the public interest. The economics of healthcare are dissimilar to other segments of the economy in several important ways, but the legal climate surrounding healthcare transactions has not yet taken all the dissimilarities into account. The laws, in effect, may need to catch up to the dynamics of the current movement toward healthcare integration.

The purpose of this chapter is to introduce you to legal perspectives on buying and selling medical practices. Four particular legal restrictions will be reviewed: antitrust laws; fraud and abuse restrictions, including the federal antikickback laws; self-referral restrictions; and the corporate practice of medicine.

ANTITRUST LAWS

If the merger or acquisition results in a substantial decrease in competition in the community, the transaction may be subject to antitrust challenge. There are three main antitrust risks to consider while forming an integrated network.

1. Price-fixing. The buyer and seller should be extremely cautious about sharing price information prior to the effective date of the merger.
2. Monopoly. They should also be careful about establishing professional fees or conducting themselves in a way that has the effect of eliminating competition after the merger.
3. Boycott. The exclusion of providers from a network can be challenged on the basis of a monopoly or a boycott.

A primary analysis of the antitrust risk should begin by asking a few questions about the proposed transaction. The first question is, What is the product market for the new service? If the merger will result in the combination of a limited array of all the specialties in the community, the antitrust risk is likely to be limited.

The second level of analysis requires a measurement of the relevant geographic market. The less expansive the geographic target service area, the less risky the transaction.

The Federal Trade Commission and the Department of Justice are most likely to focus on what happens to the distribution of market share after the merger compared to the period just prior to the merger. A mathematical index, the Hertindahl-Hirschman Index, will be applied to assure that competition is still healthy despite the merger.

Large mergers should be reported to the Attorney General and the Federal Trade Commission prior to their completion, according to federal law. Large mergers are defined as those involving sellers with $10 million in assets and buyers with $100 million in assets, or mergers involving similar amounts of annual sales.

FEDERAL ANTIKICKBACK LAWS

In 1972, Congress passed the Fraud and Abuse Act to prevent payments for referrals of patients whose services would be reimbursed under Medicare or Medicaid. The intent of the law was to protect the public from unscrupulous physicians whose judgment about the most appropriate care for their patients might be swayed by financial incentives.

The Medicare and Medicaid Antifraud Statute, 42 U.S.C. § 1320a–7b(b), prohibits: the solicitation or receipt of any remuneration of any kind, whether directly or indirectly, in return for:

a. referring a patient for the furnishing or arranging for the furnishing of any item or service for which payment may be made in whole or in part under Medicare or a state healthcare program (hereafter, Medicaid); or

b. purchasing, leasing, ordering or arranging for or recommending purchasing, leasing, or ordering any good, facility, service or item for which payment may be made in whole or in part under Medicare or Medicaid; and

the offer or payment of any remuneration of any kind, whether directly or indirectly, to induce any person to:

a. refer a patient for the furnishing or arranging for the furnishing of any item or service for which payment may be made in whole or in part under Medicare or Medicaid; or

b. to purchase, lease, order or arrange for or recommend purchasing, leasing or ordering any good, facility, service or item for which payment may be made in whole or in part by the Medicare or Medicaid programs.

The law has been interpreted quite broadly by the Inspector General and the courts, which has had the effect of causing some hospitals and medical practices to tread lightly in potential acquisitions. In an attempt to clarify the restrictions, the secretary of the Department of Health and Human Services issued regulations in 1991 describing arrangements that do not violate the act. These "Safe Harbor" regulations include provisions concerning the following issues:

1. Investment interests in large publicly traded entities
2. Investment interests in other entities
3. Lease of space or equipment
4. Personal services and management agreements
5. Sale of practice
6. Referral services
7. Employees

In 1993 the Office of the Inspector General published seven additional proposed safe harbors impacting the following:

1. Investment interests in rural areas
2. Investment interests in ambulatory surgical centers

3. Investment interests in group practices composed exclusively of active investors
4. Practitioner recruitment
5. Obstetrical malpractice insurance subsidies
6. Referral agreements for specialty services
7. Cooperative hospital service organizations

The Office of the Inspector General published final regulations in early 1996 impacting safe harbors and various managed care arrangements. The regulations reflect an attempt to ensure that regulators won't have a "chilling effect" on managed care activity. The following statement is found in the preamble to the January 1996 rules:

> Commenters (to interim rules) should not infer that because a safe harbor provision does not specifically refer to a particular arrangement or activity, it is unlawful. Nor should they interpret that lack of a safe harbor to mean that these activities will be subjected to heightened scrutiny. . . . The failure to comply with the safe harbor means only that the practice or arrangement does not have the absolute assurance of protection from antikickback liability. ("OIG revises managed care safe harbors under antikickback," *MGM Update,* March 1966, page 4.)

The escalation of acquisition activity since the publication of these two sets of safe harbors seems to indicate a growing comfort by buyers and sellers with the idea of integration without the risk of legal action under the antikickback laws. Legal challenges and future regulations will tell whether this comfort is warranted.

SELF-REFERRAL RESTRICTIONS

The most notable restrictions against self-referral are those contained in Stark I and Stark II. The Stark Laws—named for their author, California congressman Fortney H. "Pete" Stark—have become synonymous with self-referral restrictions. Stark I prohibits physicians from making a referral of a Medicare patient for clinical laboratory services to an entity with which the physician or a member of the physician's family has a financial relationship. Stark II extends the list of prohibited referrals beyond laboratory services to include the following:

    a. physical therapy

    b. occupational therapy

    c. radiology services

    d. radiation therapy services

    e. durable medical equipment

    f. parenteral and enteral nutrients, equipment, and supplies

    g. prosthetics

    h. home health services

    i. outpatient prescription drugs

    j. inpatient and outpatient hospital services

Stark I went into effect in early 1992, but the regulations for the law were not released for public comment until early 1996. Stark II prohibitions went into effect in 1995, but their regulations have yet to be produced.

The exceptions to the Stark Laws are quite notable for buyers and sellers of medical practices, and they may have unintentionally fueled the acquisition fever. Self-referrals that are *allowed* under the Stark Laws include transactions like these:

    1. Physician services personally provided by another physician practicing in the same group as the referring physician

    2. In-office ancillary services

    3. Salary payments to salaried physicians in group practices

    4. Certain employment and service agreements with hospitals

The rapid rise of acquisition activity might suggest that buyers and sellers are concluding that it is safer to join forces than to risk running afoul of the self-referral restrictions of Stark I and II.

CORPORATE PRACTICE OF MEDICINE

State statutes maintain restrictions against the practice of professional services by anyone other than a professional with a license valid in the state. Several states extend the restriction to prohibit ownership of business entities designed to deliver professional services by anyone other than the licensed professionals who practice in the business. Such restrictions, as they apply to medicine, are generally referred to as prohibitions against the "corporate practice of medicine."

These restrictions have been interpreted to limit the rights of hospitals to own physician practices in some states, but the rapidly developing dynamic of integrated health services is challenging the state statutes with regularity. Several states have recently reinterpreted their corporate practice of medicine laws to be less restrictive, and more are expected to follow suit.

CONCLUSION ABOUT LEGAL LAND MINES

While the legal risks are evident, the economics of integration are compelling buyers and sellers to wade into uncharted legal waters. Wise negotiators will consider all the legal restrictions that might impact a potential transaction before jumping headlong into a quagmire. A local healthcare attorney can be an essential partner on the negotiating team, helping both parties avert the avoidable conflicts within the law, but also finding creative solutions that build win–win strategic relationships with lasting community benefit.

6

Negotiating the Deal

NEGOTIATION IS AS IMPORTANT AS THE APPRAISAL

Reaching an agreement about the value of the practice does not in itself ensure a successful transaction. Buyers and sellers have different points of view on how to establish the value of the business. They will also likely disagree on how to execute the deal. If the acquisition or merger is intended to have longevity, the negotiation is as important as the valuation.

Successful negotiation depends on having information and on skillfully using that information to achieve your objectives. Since the possession of information is crucial to establishing a fair agreement, I recommend that the owner of the appraisal share the information with the other party. The interpretation and understanding that each party derives from the report and analysis will shape the agreement in a manner that yields the most likely opportunity for a long-term, mutually beneficial relationship.

What to Negotiate

Three major issues require negotiation in every acquisition and every merger:

1. The price and terms of the sale are first and foremost. Deciding what is to be included in the transaction and at what values is fundamental to any agreement. The appraisal focuses primarily on the disclosure of assets and values.

2. The terms of employment of the physicians after the transaction need to be negotiated simultaneously. In a merger, the employment terms translate to agreements about income distribution formulas and benefit structures.

3. Determining how decisions will be made in the new organization is the third focus of negotiations. Governance issues can impact the long-term success of the relationship just as directly as establishing the right price and having equitable employment agreements.

All three issues may be negotiated as a package, with give-and-get flowing between the parties. But each issue should be essentially balanced in its own right. That is, the buyer and the seller should each find satisfaction on each issue. They each need to be able to live with the results of the negotiation.

Price and Terms of the Sale   Auto dealers frequently tout special financing deals in which the buyer can choose between a rebate and a lower interest rate. It's a classic model for negotiating. Do you want a better price or better terms of the sale? A buyer with adequate access to cash is likely to opt for the rebate, while the buyer looking for low payments may choose the favorable interest rate. Most sales transactions have some version of the classic choice: price or terms. So too in selling a medical practice. The buyer and seller will approach the classic choice with their own perspectives, based on their own needs. If the buyer is an institution with strong reserves, they may prefer a cash purchase, avoiding unnecessary interest expense. The seller may find a windfall of cash appealing, or may prefer a revenue stream spread over a few years to reduce the tax hit.

Employment If the selling physician intends to remain in the practice as an employee, she has additional leverage in negotiating the terms of all three issues. Her continuance is an asset that carries value, which is part of the price and terms of the sale. Likewise, an employment relationship implies the need for a governance structure, and her commitment to the new employer provides an opportunity to influence how decisions will be made. The core of an employment relationship is the compensation agreement, and negotiating the base salary and incentive structure is best done at the outset of the commitment. *It is absolutely critical to have balanced interests and agreement about compensation structures.* Even if poor decisions are made on the price and terms of the sale, the long-term success of the relationship can be assured if the day-to-day motivations of the buyer and the seller are in sync.

Governance Deciding how things will get done, who has what authority, and what will happen when the system falters, is about as critical to the long-term success of the relationship as the agreement about compensation. Physicians accustomed to autonomous decision making are likely to resist a sudden switch to being accountable to someone else. The trauma of the change can be accentuated when the physician becomes accountable to a nonphysician executive. The trick to long-term success is to maintain a subtle balance between supporting the physicians' autonomy and steering them into convergence with corporate goals. Allowing physicians to be self-governing with the institution's checkbook is bound to be disastrous. But so is trying to force the high-achieving physician into compliance with a bureaucratic maze. Governance is all about balance. And that is obtained through negotiation.

Negotiating Concepts and Myths

What comes to mind when you think about negotiating? Conflict? Getting your way? Fighting for your rights? For many people, negotiating conjures images of the dreaded visit to the used-car lot, where you fear being taken advantage of. "You get what you negotiate," becomes the guiding principle, right along with "buyer beware."

Negotiating is a skill that can be learned and developed, just like communication skills. The artful negotiator pays attention to the details of what is said or not said, and researches the factors that can impact the outcome. Negotiating is the ability to resolve conflicts. It takes an intuitive sense that enables the parties to move their thinking. It also takes self-control, maintaining a healthy perspective about the importance of the issues and the outcomes, sometimes containing the urge to lash out defensively, sometimes asserting a position firmly.

The complexity of a medical practice acquisition or merger calls for artful negotiating. The local healthcare market is no place for adversarial haggling or a hostile takeover. The economic and medical well-being of communities is at stake. Buyers and sellers of medical practices should be prepared to negotiate on a higher plane, one that values the entire medical care delivery system more than an individual's agenda. We need to move from an attitude of personal primacy to an attitude of community benefit, from preserving power to sharing power.

Negotiating Skills

If reaching fair conclusions depends on negotiating, each party should spend a little time and effort brushing up on the basic negotiating skills. In this section, I'd like to discuss three of those skills, and describe how they can be used

EXHIBIT 6-1

Examples of Signaling

Statement	Signal
"I find it extremely difficult to accept your offer."	NOT IMPOSSIBLE
"We don't normally pay for goodwill."	SO WHAT'S NORMAL?
"Our lawyers advise us against anything that looks like inurement."	BUT I'LL ASK THEM
"This is our standard employment agreement."	IT'S NEGOTIABLE
"I'm not used to answering to a nonphysician."	BUT I CAN LEARN
"I'm not prepared to discuss this issue at this time."	ASK ME TOMORROW

effectively in negotiations involving medical practices. I'll concentrate on listening, self-management, and creativity.

Listening Successful negotiators learn to listen more than they talk. Listening is more than a passive exercise. Active listening involves affirming the speaker with comments, questions, and gestures. It means reading body language and expressing yourself with your posture as well as with your words. Listening in the context of negotiating also means listening to signals that the other party is moving in their understanding or negotiating posture. Exhibit 6–1 demonstrates a few examples of signals and their interpretations.

Self-Management Successful negotiators learn to control their tongue and their emotions. Antagonism weakens the negotiating position of the antagonist. Rather than lashing out in disgust at an opponent's statement, or reacting with sullen sarcasm, disciplined negotiators manage their inner feelings and respond in measured tones. You may have a gut-wrenching reaction to something the other party says or does, but you jeopardize your ability to move him from his position if you act purely on the basis of your emotional response. Instead, take a deep breath, withhold your judgment, and listen closely to discern why he said what he said, and why you felt such a strong reaction. Evaluate the situation later, if necessary, and try to put it in the perspective of the intended long-term outcome of the relationship.

Creativity Few people recognize that creativity is a skill that can be learned and developed. Perhaps even fewer use it as a negotiating tool. Creativity involves looking beyond the present circumstances for multiple right answers. People who embrace their innate innovative qualities find ways to resolve conflicts by probing deeper into the reasons for the conflicts. Unconstrained imagination draws out solutions to seemingly unresolvable differences.

A Model for Negotiating

Now that the concepts of successful negotiating have been introduced, let's take a look at a specific model for the process. The art of negotiating begins with a five-step process:

1. List your needs and the other party's needs.
2. Rank those needs in order of importance.
3. Evaluate each need in view of alternatives.
4. Look for ways to meet both needs simultaneously.
5. Consider other consequences of the proposed transaction.

1. List Needs The needs list can consist of words or short phrases that capture the concept of what is to be accomplished with the proposed transaction. For sellers, the list might include:

Income security
Freedom from management
Capital for growth
Cash for goodwill
Participation in key contracts

For the buyers, the list might look a little different:

Get referrals
Extend market share
Increase volume of patient services

Gain economies of scale
Contain costs
Participate in key contracts

2. Prioritize the Needs   Developing priorities among the needs helps to put your negotiating position into perspective. You are more likely to understand your own priorities than those of the other party, but ranking your perceptions of both parties' priorities will help you obtain a sense of the strength of your negotiating position. It may also help you understand what needs to happen to reach full agreement about the transaction. If there is agreement on both sides, for example, that participation in key contracts is the main reason for the proposed acquisition or merger, then the negotiating process is likely to be less contentious. Identifying central points of common understanding and agreement can form the foundation for discussions on less essential expectations.

Ranking the needs also helps to sort out the real reasons for the proposed transaction. If the seller can only identify a vague need to affiliate because his colleagues are doing so, this step in the negotiating process may evoke a clarification of the reasons, or expose the weakness of the potential combination.

3. Evaluate the Alternatives   This requires the proverbial "walking in the other's moccasins" exercise. You need to try placing yourself in the position of the other party, and honestly consider how they might get their needs met if you do not agree to the proposed transaction. If you are the seller, think about how the buyers might elect to acquire a competitor practice or recruit a physician and develop a new practice. If you are the buyer, consider who else the practice might sell to, or how the owners might get access to capital for growth without tapping into your resources.

4. Look for Mutual Satisfaction   Agreement may require compromise on the part of both the buyers and the sellers. Look for creative ways to get your needs met while helping the other party get their needs met. Creativity is the key to this process. You need to look beyond traditions and conventional wisdom and delve into a wide variety of alternatives to find mutually beneficial points of agreement. Some examples:

■ Perhaps the cash for goodwill can be paid over an extended period of time, based on the seller's commitment to assist in physician recruitment.

■ Consider how freedom from management can help the seller increase referrals through higher volumes of patient care.

■ Evaluate the benefit of holding physicians accountable for containing costs as a part of their compensation incentive.

■ Base compensation growth on successful participation in managed care contracts.

5. Consider other Consequences   Every relationship has the potential for unintended consequences. The implications of those consequences may be good or bad, but they should be considered and anticipated in the negotiation process. Here is a partial list of consequences to consider:

■ Examine the precedent of acquiring/selling the practice. Who else is likely to follow suit? What might the impact of the precedent be? If you represent a hospital, will you have the capital required to answer the requests of other physicians to be acquired under similar terms?

■ Will the physicians still have a balanced incentive to perform? "Retirement on the job" can occur if the former entrepreneur is cashed out and no longer shoulders the business risk that once was routine.

■ How might competitors respond? Will this invite competition or incite a price war for other practice acquisitions?

■ Will the market shift because of this new relationship? What other moves might be required to complete the desired market shift or avert an outflow of market share?

■ What if reimbursement patterns change significantly? What assumptions am I banking on to achieve long-term success in this new relationship?

■ Who might be offended by this new business relationship, and how might that impact us? How will referral patterns change that have been based on trust and independence?

■ What will happen if the venture turns sour? Should there be a provision for getting out of the relationship before the terms of payment have concluded?

SUCCESSFUL NEGOTIATION IS BASED ON TRUST

Successful negotiation requires information and interpretation, to be sure. But it also requires mutual respect and trust. A business transaction that is based on legal agreements exclusive of trust is doomed to contention at best, and failure at worst. After every I is dotted and every T crossed, the relationship will still encounter questions that require answers months and years down the road. Those answers can make or break the mutual benefit intended by the acquisition or merger, and they can be answered well only if the interest of each party is balanced by trust.

7

C H A P T E R

Tax Considerations

Tax laws can impact the net result of a practice acquisition in significant ways. Buyers and sellers who wisely anticipate the tax consequences of the proposed transaction improve their negotiating positions and help set the stage for a no-surprises relationship. Ignoring the tax angles can cause a congenial relationship to sour quickly when the IRS takes an excessive portion of the sales proceeds, a portion that could have been reduced through sound tax planning.

The consequences are important for both buyers and sellers. The benefits received by the seller are likely to be taxed at various rates according to the wording of the contracts and the structure of the relationship. But the Internal Revenue Service is also interested in the implications of the transaction for the buyer.

Of course, the details of every transaction will require local review by qualified professionals. Engaging your CPA or tax attorney early in the negotiations can prevent headaches later. Local tax advisors can keep you abreast of both state and federal requirements, minimizing the tax bites of both agencies. The circumstances of any particular transaction may also vary according to the legal construction of both the buyer and the seller.

TAX OBJECTIVES FOR BUYERS AND SELLERS

The primary goal for sellers in structuring the transaction should be to shift as much of the proceeds as possible to capital gains rather than ordinary income. Every dollar shifted to capital gains will be taxed at a lower rate, currently 28 percent, instead of the ordinary income tax rates, currently 36 or 39.6 percent. State tax laws also usually offer favorable rates for capital gains.

The primary goal for buyers in structuring a tax-wise transaction is to avoid drawing the attention of the IRS and triggering an audit or other action. An astute buyer will work for ways to balance the needs of both parties, minimizing his own risk for scrutiny while minimizing the seller's tax consequences.

The best time to determine the tax consequences of a transaction is after a value has been determined, but before that value is allocated to specific components. There are no firm allocation rules beyond the actions' being reasonable and defendable. The more that can be allocated to capital gains, the better the result for the seller.

Let's take a look at each of the potential components of a transaction in light of the tax consequences for the seller.

Furniture and Equipment

The value of furniture and equipment can be segregated into three components for tax purposes.

1. The depreciated value or net book value
2. The difference between the original cost and the depreciated value
3. Amounts in excess of original cost

Revenues the seller receives to cover the first portion will not be considered taxable income. Revenues allocated to the second portion, however, will be taxed as ordinary income. The seller has already gained the benefit of a tax break for depreciation for this amount, so any revenue in excess of net book value is "recaptured depreciation," which is considered ordinary income and is taxed at the higher rates. Only amounts received beyond the original cost would be considered capital gains.

In some states, sales taxes may apply to the purchase of used furniture and equipment. These taxes will most likely be the responsibility of the buyer, but the tax costs may become a variable in the negotiation of the total value of the practice.

Leasehold improvements are treated differently than other assets. They are usually written off slowly, over 39 or 31.5 years, depending on when the building they are part of was purchased. But when you sell your practice, you are allowed to deduct all the remaining leasehold improvement write-off in the year of the sale. Let's consider, for example, a leasehold improvement of $50,000 made three years ago. You may have written off $4,000, but a sale of the practice can trigger a deduction of the remaining $46,000 the year the sale is completed.

Real Estate

If the medical office building is part of the transaction, the amount paid in excess of the base cost will be taxed at the capital gains rate, just as furniture and equipment is treated. The base cost is the original cost plus the cost of improvements. Recaptured depreciation will be recognized as ordinary income.

The complexities of the tax laws have generally treated real estate more favorably than professional service corporations. This has led to the predominant practice of holding real estate in a separate real estate partnership, even if it is owned by the same people who are stockholders in the professional corporation. Including real estate in the acquisition of the practice can get complicated, especially when the partnership and the corporation are not made up of identical owners. If the location and configuration of the real estate is an integral part of the value of the practice, it is worth working through these complexities. But sometimes it may be simpler, and less costly, for the buyer to acquire the practice, minus the real estate, and move to another location.

Accounts Receivable

Payments for accounts receivable will be treated as ordinary income. The tax liability might be reduced slightly by having them appraised for collectibility. If it is clear that you will only collect a portion of the receivables because of their age, contractual discounts, and historical collection patterns, it is reasonable to reduce the value attributed to them, and reduce the tax bite at the same time.

Goodwill

Goodwill is generally considered a capital gain, so from the seller's tax-wise perspective, the transaction should be weighted toward goodwill. The seller can benefit even more if the payment for goodwill is spread over several years, thereby deferring some of the tax burden to future years when the money is actually received. But paying for goodwill may cause other complications for buyers, so this is an area for careful negotiation.

If the buyer is a hospital concerned about charges of inurement, they may not want to appear to be paying heavily for goodwill. Recent IRS decisions have reintroduced a spirit of caution in the hospital community. A Texas hospital was fined for its generous recruitment practices and a Florida facility lost its tax-exempt status on the grounds that it paid too much for medical practices it acquired. While these cautionary tales may not concern the physicians looking for a good deal, they must be understood because they are likely to shape the negotiating posture of nervous hospital executives.

A for-profit buyer might also balk at paying significant portions of the total value for goodwill, but for other reasons. The for-profit company can depreciate the goodwill, but slowly, over a period of 15 years. They can depreciate furniture and equipment much faster, and therefore might be more interested in allocating a larger portion of the total negotiated value to those items.

The other legal constraints explored in Chapter 4 are also likely to enter into discussions about the tax treatment of the proposed transaction. If paying for goodwill puts the hospital in jeopardy for charges of fraud and abuse, kickbacks, or private inurement, physicians will have to find other ways to negotiate the value of their practices. If the physician insists on structuring a deal for the seller's best tax advantage, only to place the buyer at risk for far more important issues, he faces the possibility of losing the deal altogether.

Stock

Value received for stock is considered a capital gain, to the extent that it exceeds the price paid for stock when the physician bought in. If the practice was started by the physician, the entire amount allocated for stock might be considered a capital gain. But if a physician bought into a group for $3 per share, and the group sells at $8 per share, the physician will face a capital gain on the difference, $5 per share times the number of shares he or she holds.

The problem is that most buyers aren't interested in owning the stock of a professional corporation. They generally seek to buy the assets, which can be depreciated, rather than stock (which can't), and employ the physicians. Another reason why stock isn't of interest is that when one company buys another, the buyer typically acquires the liabilities along with the equity.

Covenant Not to Compete

A covenant not to compete may have value similar to good-will, but without some of the risks outlined in Chapter 5. It can be treated as a capital gains tax event, but the seller must be sure he's willing to abide by the conditions of the contract. Agreeing not to compete most likely means having to move out of the area. The tax treatment of payment for a covenant not to compete might be favorable, but it comes with a social and professional cost that must be balanced.

Compensation

If the seller is going to work for the buyer, some of the value of the practice can be deferred in the form of future compensation or a signing bonus. The seller will have to pay taxes on these amounts as ordinary income, but the concept offers a degree of flexibility for structuring the cash-flow needs of the buyer.

DOUBLE TAXATION

One of the biggest problems facing sellers of a professional corporation is the double taxation dilemma. Any profit showing on the corporation's financial statement at the close of the fiscal year is taxed at the corporate tax rate, currently 35 percent from dollar one. If the corporation incurs a massive surge in cash in one year due to the acquisition, and all the extra cash is suddenly paid as income to the seller, the IRS could argue that the compensation is excessive, and that the corporation should have paid its share of taxes first. That could mean paying 35 percent for corporate taxes, then paying another 28 percent or more on what is left as ordinary income.

Physicians can employ a great defensive strategy by setting up a deferred compensation plan within the corporation, well in advance of an acquisition. By setting up a "golden parachute," the seller can direct the excess cash from the proceeds of a sale without having a lengthy argument with the IRS. Establishing a deferred compensation plan at the last minute may draw fire, but having one in place a year or more in advance of needing it can enable the seller to protect more of the proceeds from income taxes.

OTHER ISSUES CONCERNING TAXES

Retirement Plans

Medical practices with established retirement plans face additional tax questions when they are acquired. Merging retirement plans can be complicated. If the rules of the buyer's plan are different from the rules of the seller's plan, blending the two becomes a risky process in the eyes of the IRS.

The simplest solution is for the seller to dissolve her plan according to its own rules, and distribute the proceeds to herself and her employees as a rollover independent retirement account (IRA). If the plan rules allow for direct distributions to employees upon the dissolution of the plan, be sure to follow the IRS requirements for withholding tax on the lump sum distributions, and depositing it with payroll taxes.

Terms of the Sale

A single large payment to the seller is likely to trigger the greatest tax consequences, while paying for the acquisition over time has two benefits. Periodic payments over a series of years can defer some of the tax consequences, and may place the physician in a lower tax bracket for those periods. Spreading payments over time to a physician who remains employed by the buyer also helps to keep the employment relationship strong. The physician is less likely to "retire on the job," knowing that future payments may depend on maintaining the vitality of the practice.

8

CHAPTER

Understanding the Due Diligence Process

DUE DILIGENCE DEFINED

The legal and moral foundation of business relationships includes the assumption that each party will deal with the other fairly and honestly. That assumption is verified through the "due diligence" process, in which the buyer obtains documentation to support the seller's claims about the value of the business. This is particularly important when the buyer is a trustee of assets that are not personally owned, such as in the case for an executive of a not-for-profit hospital. Every wise purchaser, however, will want to validate the responsible use of resources in a major transaction such as the acquisition of a medical practice. The primary purpose of due diligence is to expose the risks and liabilities associated with ownership of the business.

WHAT THE SELLER MUST EXPOSE AND WHEN

The seller is expected to fully disclose material information that may affect the buyer's risk, according to the principles of fair dealing. If an appraisal is conducted, the appraiser should answer the buyer's need for information at the time that a valuation conclusion is reached. If an appraisal is not completed, the seller should disclose all material information about the ownership of the business prior to reaching an agreement on the price and terms of the transaction.

The information that might be considered material to the transaction may include some or all of the following:

- Financial statements
- Tax records
- Bank statements
- Leases on property or equipment
- Debts or other liabilities of the practice
- Patient payment records
- Patient medical records
- Documentation of any legal actions taken by or against the practice
- Information about pending or threatened legal action
- Documentation of compliance with regulatory agencies
- Information about any actions against the practice by regulatory agencies

Exibit 8–1 is a due diligence checklist highlighting these and other data requirements.

EXHIBIT 8-1

Due Diligence Checklist

The following information should be reviewed prior to entering a legal relationship with a medical practice:

_____ Federal, state, and local tax returns for each of the past five fiscal years

_____ Financial statements compiled by the practice or its CPA firm for each of the last five fiscal years

_____ Physicians' W-2 statements for each of the past five fiscal years

_____ Most recent monthly financial statement with year-to-date information

_____ Production reports showing procedures and charges by physician for the past five years, plus current year-to-date data

_____ Office visit volumes by physician for each of the past five years

_____ Charges, payments, and adjustments by physician and payer type for the current fiscal year

_____ The most recent tabulation of the aged accounts receivable by payer type

_____ The current fee schedule by CPT code

_____ An estimate of the number of all active and inactive patient charts

_____ A list of all employees by position, average weekly schedule, and wage

_____ A copy of personnel policies and of all written job descriptions

_____ A copy of written credit and collection policies

_____ A copy of all lease agreements on offices and equipment

_____ The depreciation schedule for all owned equipment

_____ A list and explanation of all debts of the practice

_____ A list of all equipment and supplies owned by the practice, with appraisal at fair market value

_____ Perspectives gained from interviews of each provider and key staff member regarding the working culture of the office, the characteristics of the patients, and the effectiveness of the management

CONFIDENTIALITY

Information discovered about a business in the course of an appraisal is potentially powerful. The appraiser may discover potential for business development that the current owners have not recognized, and that information could be exploited by an unscrupulous competitor in a way that could harm the business owner. If information is not handled in a confidential manner and used for the purpose for which it is intended, the potential for damage to professional reputations and to successful business relationships can be enormous. For that reason, many physicians insist on securing a legal agreement that requires both parties in a potential transaction to hold business and professional information confidential. If either party breaks confidentiality, causing harm to the other, the agreement can spell out the recourse the damaged party can follow to recover the losses.

The damage to fragile trust relationships, however, may not be recoverable. Jeff Goldsmith, Ph.D., described the integration of private practices as "a little like driving a truck loaded with nitroglycerin along a bumpy road." (*Healthcare Forum Journal*) Exercising due diligence and agreeing to the principles of confidentiality will not ensure the protection of business interests unless trust is an integral part of the relationship.

Exhibit 8–2 offers a suggested format for a confidentiality statement. The specific circumstances of a proposed transaction should also be reviewed by an attorney to ensure their compliance with local laws.

EXHIBIT 8–2

Sample Confidentiality Statement

NONDISCLOSURE/COMPETITION AGREEMENT

THIS AGREEMENT entered into the _____ day of _____ 199X, by and between _____ , P.C., a professional corporation (SELLER), whose business address is _____ , and _____ , a corporation (BUYER), whose business address is _____ .

WITNESSETH

WHEREAS, ___(BUYER)___ and ___(SELLER)___ desire to negotiate terms for a business relationship; and

WHEREAS, in the course of said negotiations, ___(BUYER)___ and ___(SELLER)___ shall exchange confidential information relating to financial and business operations;

NOW, THEREFORE, in consideration of the mutual benefits contained herein, and in order to induce the Parties to use their best efforts toward successful negotiations, ___(BUYER)___ and ___(SELLER)___ agree as follows:

I. BUYER COMMITMENTS

A. Proprietary Information ___(BUYER)___ agrees that it will not directly or indirectly disclose to any person, entity, firm, or company, except _____ , or use to its own benefit or the benefit of any other person, entity, firm, or company, except _____ , directly or indirectly in competition with ___(SELLER)___ , any knowledge or information of any kind concerning any matters affecting or relating to the business of ___(SELLER)___ , or any other information concerning ___(SELLER)___ 's business, its manner of operation, or its clients, plans, methods of operation, techniques, or other data or business information of any kind, nature, or description as contained in any policy, procedure manuals, or written correspondence or documents provided to ___(BUYER)___ . ___(BUYER)___ shall, upon conclusion of negotiations, retain all books, records, notes, and financial information obtained in the course of the project.

B. NonInterference ___(BUYER)___ agrees that it shall not solicit, directly or indirectly, any facility serviced by ___(SELLER)___ to provide like professional services and shall not attempt to persuade a facility at which ___(SELLER)___ has contractual agreements to terminate or breach its contract with ___(SELLER)___ .

(continued)

E X H I B I T   8 – 2 — *Concluded*

Sample Confidentiality Statement

___(BUYER)___ agrees that in addition to any other limitation, for a period of one (1) year after the conclusion of negotiations, it will not directly or indirectly assist any individual or corporation in contacting any facilities or physicians' groups with which ___(SELLER)___ has an existing contract, or in any other way attempt to convince any current (SELLER) contracted facility to cancel such contract.

II. SELLER COMMITMENTS

A. Full Disclosure ___(SELLER)___ agrees to comply with any and all requests for information presented by ___(BUYER)___ during the course of the negotiations, and to answer any and all questions truthfully and completely.

IN WITNESS WHEREOF, this agreement has been duly executed by the parties hereto as of the date first above written.

SELLER   BUYER

_____   _____

President   President

9
CHAPTER

Before Signing the Contract or Agreement

Reaching an agreement can be a thrill. For the physician who is selling, the agreement can represent the fulfillment of a lifelong dream. The buyer can find deep satisfaction, as well, in finalizing a deal that carries importance beyond the initial transaction. It may mean extending the market share and influence of the organization, or taking a key step toward vertical integration and stronger competitiveness, or perhaps it can mean a career advancement for the executive who closes the deal.

It may be easy, in the thrill of victory, to ignore details critical to the long-term success of the business relationship. This chapter can be viewed as a kind of checklist of those details; a litany of decisions and implications to think of on both sides of the transaction, any one of which could cause distress down the road. Think of it as the kind of checklist a pilot goes through before taking off, making sure the trip will be a safe one.

PROTECTIVE COVENANTS FOR BUYERS

As with any purchase, *caveat emptor* applies: buyer beware. The buyer should make sure the agreements address the issues that are important to him, not just in the next few months, but for the long-term success of the relationship. Each issue should be fully discussed and the agreements committed to writing. The issues discussed in the following sections relate mostly to employment of the physician whose practice is acquired.

Full Disclosure   The buyer has a right to believe that the seller has been fully honest in disclosing information that is material in determining the value of the business and the intentions of the seller. If material information is withheld, the buyer should have some means of recourse, even to the extent of nullifying the deal, within a reasonable period of time.

Maintaining Licensure, Insurability, and Privileges   If the buyer plans to employ the seller, the agreement should spell out the assumptions about the physician's ability to practice as intended. Without a medical license, professional liability insurance, or hospital privileges, the physician would be hard-pressed to continue in employment, and the long-term value of the practice goodwill would rapidly diminish.

Physician's Full Effort   One of the most common risks hospitals face in employing a physician after buying her practice is that the physician loses interest in working as hard as she did when she bore the full risk and reward of business pressure. The newly employed physician might find it convenient to take on new assignments that don't benefit the new employer, such as precepting residents, writing a book, lecturing, or moonlighting at a community clinic. The agreement should clarify who can decide which assignments to accept, and when, and who receives honoraria when they are offered.

Production Standards   Perhaps the most powerful component of an employment agreement will be the clause describing the incentive structure. Physicians who work under salaries need to know what is expected of them to maintain the agreed level of compensation. They should also know how their productivity will be monitored, and how they will receive feedback about their performance on a regular basis. I generally find that physicians respond to data very well. They look for ways to meet or exceed others' expectations, perhaps driven by the same discipline that brought them through medical training programs. Production standards should be a cornerstone of the relationship and they should be negotiated early in the agreement.

Accountability   The employed physician should know who will supervise him. Supervision doesn't need to be performed by another physician, although complying with medical peer review can and should be part of the expected standard of performance. I have encountered several physicians in employment relationships who could not tell me who their supervisor was, and the confusion that resulted caused financial and other hardships for the institution that invested in the acquisition of the practice.

Noncompetition   Since goodwill is at least partially nonseverable from the physician, the buyer should require that the physician cannot leave within a short time and establish a competitive practice within the immediate area. If the buyer is paying for the loyalty of patients to the practice, that loyalty should be protected as any other investment would be. The courts are divided on defining reasonable expectations for noncompetition, so local advisors should be consulted.

Length of the Employment Contract   The buyer should carefully consider how long the initial employment agreement should last. If there is reason to believe a long-term relationship may be undesirable, the agreement can be structured for only one or two years. Three to five years is more common, however, and will help to ensure the stabilization and growth of the practice during the sensitive transition period.

Length of Notice upon Termination   Buyers can further protect their interests by requiring a modestly lengthy notice upon termination of employment, typically three months or more. If the physician finds it easy to leave, she will have less incentive to stay. If she must work for three months in uncomfortable circumstances, she may be more inclined to work out the differences and comply with the employer's expectations. If the employed physician does give three months' notice of termination, the employer has a better chance of replacing her with a new recruit than if only one month's notice is tendered.

PROTECTIVE COVENANTS FOR SELLERS

Timely Payments   Sellers should expect to be paid the agreed amounts at the agreed times, and to have a recourse if the buyer breaches the contract. Payments may be spread over time for tax purposes, but specific dates and amounts should be determined in writing at the time of the agreement.

Professional Autonomy for Patient Care   Institutional employers may have authority over much of a physician's performance, but decisions about which patients need what kind of care should remain the prerogative of the physician, within the professional standards of care for the specialty and consistent with the rules of participating healthcare plans.

Length of the Employment Contract   The seller will need to gauge his level of comfort with the buyer, and negotiate the term of employment accordingly. Any material intent to leave within the term of the agreement should, of course, be disclosed. Establishing a comfortable length for the employment term can help the physician be secure while also keeping a degree of flexibility.

Length of Notice upon Termination   The seller may want to keep the notice requirement relatively short to ensure maximum flexibility, but there is a benefit to a more lengthy notice period. If the employment agreement is terminated by the employer, the length of notice requirement becomes a severance agreement, assuring a continuance of income until the physician can secure other employment.

Sharing of Information   A common complaint of hospital-employed physicians is that they do not feel they are kept well-informed about the decisions impacting their practice, their productivity, the effect of negotiations with healthcare plans, or the hospital's strategic direction. Protection for the physician's right to know can be built into the agreement, detailing the communication expectations for maintaining a healthy relationship.

Backing Out   Some physicians with successful histories as practice owners have difficulty making the adjustment to employment. For those concerned about the transition, I recommend developing a means for the physician to buy her practice back, within a limited period of time, on predetermined terms. A simple provision like this can offer the security needed to face an unknown transition, and that security can contribute to an even more successful long-term employment relationship.

ASSUMING LIABILITIES

There are three particular areas of liability that require review and decisions in the acquisition process above and beyond the discussions about liabilities appearing on the balance sheet. Decisions are required on professional liability insurance, staff employment issues, and reimbursement issues.

Professional Liability Insurance   Professional liability insurance policies are not all alike, and the differences can have a major impact on the negotiating process. Insurance can be a key to a physician's security, so maintaining a strong professional liability policy can contribute to building trust in the new relationship. Decisions are required in the following areas:

■ Who will be the new carrier? The policies generally go with the practitioner, so if the new carrier is different from the current carrier, a new application and credentialing process is likely to be required. The physician will need to be assured that the new carrier is solid and trustworthy, and that any differences in the premiums will not impact his income negatively.

■ What will be the type and level of coverage? The two major types of professional liability insurance are claims-made and occurrence. Claims-made policies generally are less expensive, but they may require a fee, called a "tail," if the physician changes policies within a particular time period. The agreement should address who will take responsibility for the tail under various circumstances.

■ Who has the right to binding arbitration? Many carriers offer discounts if they retain the right to binding arbitration. Some physicians may find it offensive to relinquish their right to decide when to arbitrate and when to fight, so clarity about this issue is important before the agreement is signed.

■ When does the new coverage begin? For physician security, it is imperative that no lapse of coverage occur. To be safe, a few days' overlap might be wise.

Staff Employment Issues   Physicians can be protective of their staff's interests, and rightly so. The staff may be the most vulnerable parties to the acquisition. They may not have any input to the decision process, and their employment security may be at stake. Sensitivity to their needs and expectations can make the transition smooth, and insensitivity can cause a well-constructed plan to stumble. Here are a few of the decisions required:

■ What will happen to the benefit structure? The new employer will need to carefully plan benefits that balance the long-term interests of the practice with the short-term needs for maintaining staff loyalty and patient flow. It may be necessary to "grandfather" selected employees into an existing longevity grid that rewards them on the basis of their experience and time with the practice. On the other hand, if the former practice was hampered by overgenerous benefits, the acquisition may be an opportunity to restructure the compensation and benefit plan to better reflect the marketplace.

Two particular benefits to examine are the sick leave and vacation plans. Employees may have accrued time that they expect to receive, either in time off or in cash. Most practices do not accrue these values as liabilities on their balance sheets, but they can later become painful realizations if they are ignored at the time of an acquisition.

■ What will happen to existing retirement plans? The difficulties associated with blending two complicated, and highly regulated, retirement plans represent a liability that calls for decisions up front. Most acquisitions result in the closure of the former retirement plan, with distributions to the rollover Individual Retirement Account of the employee's choice.

■ How secure will my job be? This is perhaps the most difficult question to face, because the answer may be different for each employee. Employment transitions are never easy, and meeting the needs and expectations of several anxious employees at once can drain energy and time from patient care. One of the more conservative approaches is to negotiate a "safe" transition period of 6 to 12 months, during which the new employer can sort out what the long-term staffing needs of the practice may be, and who should fill those positions. The transition period is also a time for employees to sort out their satisfaction with their new employer, and potentially their new co-workers.

Reimbursement Issues   Practice acquisitions also carry implications for physician reimbursement that cannot be ignored. The following three issues are key:

■ What new credentialing will be required? Many insurance companies require physicians who change the ownership of their practice, or who move to employment, to report the event and apply for a different provider identification number. If the transition also includes a move to a new address, the Drug Enforcement Administration will need to know as well. The process of recredentialing can take from a few weeks to several months, and payments can be slowed down or deferred until the new provider identification numbers are all in place. The new employer, who will most likely be at financial risk, should anticipate the recredentialing needs and get an early start to reduce the risk of cash slowdowns.

■ Who will assume the liability for an audit of pre-transition reimbursement patterns? Audits can occur years after a questionable transaction takes place. New owners will likely be required to comply with auditors' requests for information, but the liability for penalties should be negotiated before the chance of an audit occurs. In most cases, the former owner will remain liable for his actions, even if he is no longer responsible for a practice that made mistakes under his ownership.

■ Who will be responsible for collecting the old accounts receivable? If the accounts receivable are purchased outright, then of course the new owner is responsible for their collection. But if they are not part of the deal, the seller may need to negotiate a service fee for staff and computer resources for the new owner to continue to work the old accounts receivable and forward the net receipts to the seller. Service bureaus typically charge from 6 to 10 percent for collecting accounts receivable, until they require collection agency attention. The negotiating might begin in that range, or the seller may elect to send all her old accounts receivable to an outside agency.

FINE PRINT

No checklist can anticipate every issue that might cause difficulties in the posttransition period, but buyers and sellers should look for potential glitches that might be found "between the lines." Ask yourself what assumptions you are making about the long-term relationship. Test those assumptions through your discussions, and draw examples of potential scenarios for ambiguous situations. I find this technique to be of particular help in laying out the compensation expectations. If compensation is based in part on productivity, develop examples of what might transpire, based on historical data or on projections incorporating new assumptions. Both sides should feel comfortable with the assumptions and with realistic expectations made by the other. You are each making claims upon the other. Be sure your trust is well placed, and your chances of disappointment will be minimized.

10

CHAPTER

Life after the Deal

One of the most difficult, and most critical, aspects of buying or selling a medical practice is to anticipate what life will be like after the deal is consummated. The thrill of the hunt for both the buyer and the seller can be short-lived if disappointment sets in after just a few months. Remorse can hit both the buyer and the seller, and in the worst case, cause a potentially positive relationship to turn negative.

The purpose of this chapter is to sensitize both parties to think about the ramifications of their decisions in the months and years following the transaction. If the implications of the new relationship can be visualized early on, the negotiations may go smoother, the deal may be fairer, and both parties may be more likely to get what they want from the relationship in the long term. Visualizing a positive outcome helps achieve a win–win relationship.

This discussion will focus on four parts of that vision. I will examine how decisions will get made, how to blend cultures, how to prepare for market changes, and how to maintain economic soundness after the deal is done.

HOW DECISIONS GET MADE

Governance of a solo practice is a relatively simple process. The owner makes all the clinical and business decisions, sometimes with the input of her staff. Qualified and competent staff may be assigned responsibility for particular decisions once they have earned the trust of the owner.

Governing a small group practice is slightly more complex. The physician-owners usually work toward a unanimous consensus on most business issues through a deliberative process. As groups grow, they typically engage a manager to handle most of the routine decisions and to supervise the staff. But even with competent management in place, physicians retain the authority to make policy decisions that impact the strategic direction of the practice.

As groups grow beyond a dozen physicians, the consensus-building process may give way to delegation of decision-making authority to an executive committee. Board meetings are more likely to result in voting records that include split decisions. Unanimity may give way to majority-controlled decisions, along with a degree of political maneuvering.

Institutions such as hospitals are typically governed quite differently from most small medical groups. They are larger bureaucracies that rely on centralized authority, chains of command, and departmentalization of specific functions. When institutions acquire small medical practices, the environment could not be riper for a clash of cultures. The decisions on which the physicians forged a consensus are now segregated to various departments, which are headed by managers who try to conform the practice to fit their experience. Thus purchasing routine supplies for the medical practice can become a multistep process, complete with red tape; the interpretation of employee policies can become more rigid; and budgets begin to be used as a battleground for power.

Buyers and sellers are wise to set the stage for efficient and effective decision making. The buyer generally has the right to make the rules for decision making, but the buyer should also do what it takes to make those rules clear and easy to follow. Sellers will need to learn to comply with the rules, and to understand what will happen to them when the rules are not followed. That means more than simply showing the physician the organizational chart. It means introducing him and his office staff to the people that will serve them, giving them a chance to ask questions of each other and get acquainted, at least on a professional level. It means detailing who needs to make which decisions and what spending authority is granted to whom to make things happen.

The following specific decision areas should be anticipated:

- Employment Issues. Who will have the authority to hire, fire, and supervise? Who sets wage and benefit policies? Who interprets policies when questions arise? What happens when there is a disagreement about how many staff are needed?

- Patient Policies. Who decides what the patient payer mix should be? Who handles patient complaints? How much authority does the physician have to give professional courtesy? Who sets the office hours?

- Fees. Who sets the fee schedule? Who monitors reimbursement patterns to identify opportunities for raising fees? How will new procedures be priced? Do we use a single fee schedule or multiple schedules?

- Contracts. Which insurance and managed care contracts will the practice participate in? Who will decide? How do we handle maintenance contracts for software and equipment? Who signs the lease?

- Equipment Purchases. Who will decide what to buy when? Where do we go to shop for new equipment? What spending limits need to be set for purchases? What grade of furniture is needed?

■ Supply Purchases. How do we get routine supplies? How much inventory do we need to keep on hand? Where can we store excess inventory purchased in quantity for best pricing?

■ Medical Billing. *(This issue is absolutely critical.)* Who will be responsible for our billing? What will we need to know to keep billings current? How can we be assured that billing is being done competently and that reimbursement is optimized? If new systems are required, how will the staff be trained? What reports will we see monthly to monitor our performance?

BLENDING CULTURES

Blending unlike corporate cultures can be like an arranged marriage. The two parties can become like one, but only by making a commitment to each other and by communicating fully over time. The relationship can bloom and grow if it is based on mutual respect, similar values, and complementary needs. The negotiating process needs to give way to a more complete blending of cultures through the steps outlined in the following paragraphs.

Understanding Mutual Needs

Blending begins by listening to each other. As the buyer listens to the seller's needs and the seller hears the buyer's concerns, they begin to see how they can each be part of the solution for the other. This kind of understanding can come only when both sides are ready to set aside their biases and really listen. Active listening calls for honesty, feedback, clarification, and verification.

If a physician is interested in selling his practice only to get the top dollar for his goodwill, he may not be a good candidate for an institution to buy. But if he is interested in positioning his practice for success in managed care, and he sees what the institution can do to help him achieve that goal, both parties have a greater chance of succeeding.

Understanding Differences between Large and Small Organizations

The differences in governance between large and small organizations have already been addressed. But the differences may go much deeper. Small-practice physicians have elected a lifestyle that suits their personalities. Changing organizations may require some adjustment to their independent thinking and to their personality profile. Wise executives will recognize the value of the small organization, its ability to move quickly, its responsiveness to market forces, and its ability to serve people with a personal style. Wise physicians will see the value in the larger organization's ability to obtain access to capital, to apply political strength, and to keep an eye to the future. Understanding these differences can lead to leveraging them.

Grieving the Loss of Control

For some physicians, the move away from full control of their practices will be shocking. The loss of control can take an emotional toll, just as the loss of a loved one can do. Executives who are sensitive to this loss can help physicians by allowing them to grieve in a natural way.

The grief process involves stages. When the shock of loss is first felt, the physician may react with denial. Denial gives way to anger, then sadness. In the latter stages, the physician will be willing to negotiate, then accept the changes imposed upon her.

These stages may be evident in physicians as they face the adjustments to managed care models as well as the adjustment to affiliations with other organizations. Those who vehemently deny the effects of managed care are most at risk of being consumed by it. Those who show signs of moving toward acceptance of the change may be some of the most successful partners in integrated systems.

Identifying Issues of Common Destiny

Few things draw people together as effectively as a common destiny or a common enemy. Physicians and hospitals may find both to be reasonable arguments for their cooperation. A positive outlook about how the two organizations can be more effective together rather than apart can be a powerful motivator for affiliation. Likewise, a negative outlook about what competitors or managed care forces can do to them can compel unlikely partners to work in a healthy relationship.

I think it is important to note that physicians and hospitals have historically had love–hate relationships. It is not reasonable for 60 years of rivalry to simply give way to collegiality without some degree of rancor. Change is hard, but politics makes for strange bedfellows. Focusing on the reasons for blending cultures can help immensely to overcome the obstacles.

Forming the New Team

After all the discussion about blending cultures, the key will be found in the people that form a new team of inter-dependent colleagues. It takes individual personalities working together on a regular basis to solve operational problems, resolve philosophical differences, negotiate poli-cies, monitor progress, and hold one another accountable. Success can rise from the blend of a small team committed to mutual goals, fortified with a positive attitude.

I recommend forming a transition team of no more than five people from both organizations; perhaps three from the buyer and two from the seller. Their assignment should be to build a consensus on all the critical issues outlined in Chapters 8 and 9, then to set the agenda for developing the practice in ways that are consistent with the reasons for the acquisition. The individuals should be selected not only for their knowledge and competence in getting things done, but also for their personalities, repre-senting organizational balance and integrity.

PREPARING FOR MARKET CHANGES

Once the transition has been accomplished and the adjustments to the new relationship are well under way, the integrated system should turn its attention toward preparing for the future.

Information Systems

The future of managed care will depend on physicians' ability to manage information. The leadership of the integrated system will need to begin to define the kind of information the practice will need to manage, the infrastructure required to gather and analyze that information, and the reports that will be essential to managing the care of larger groups of people.

Many institutions may be oriented toward simply blending the medical practice computer systems with their own in the hopes of gaining economies of scale and in the name of integrating information systems. Blending institutional information systems with those of medical practices should be done very carefully and thoughtfully. The needs of the organizations may be quite different, both now and in the future, and those differences may call for alternative information systems.

Practice Efficiency

The blended organization should examine its opportunities for cutting costs. Successful competitors in the managed care market are those who can deliver excellent care at an excellent price. Cost cutting is one answer, but it must be done carefully. If the seller sees the buyer as managing with a machete, the trust built throughout the negotiating process may be threatened. But if cost cutting comes through prudent purchasing, eliminating wasted steps, and enhancing the productivity of the staff with technology, the bottom-line results can have a lasting positive impact on competitiveness.

Engaging a management consultant in the early stages of integration can be a wise investment. Skilled consultants can identify opportunities for cost cutting and for revenue enhancement, and can be a valuable resource in mediating the blending of cultures.

Customer Service Improvement

Preparing the practice for the consumer-oriented market of the future will also call for improving the services, from swift answers to telephone calls to shortening waiting times. As patients are faced with more choices for their medical care, they are likely to be attracted to those that are most sensitive to their preferences. Market-responsive strategies may include staff training, instituting patient satisfaction surveys, developing word-of-mouth marketing campaigns, and establishing patient response hot lines for managing complaints.

Improving customer service may also include efforts to help physicians be more sensitive to patients. The integrated system may initiate a peer review system to help physicians learn from one another, improving both their clinical judgment and their patient responsiveness.

Discerning Best Strategies

Each physician involved in an integrated system should understand his role and should play a part in developing a competitive strategy for the system. Physicians are frequently the closest to the patient-customer. Executives may be closer to the employer-customer or the insurer-customer. Both physicians and executives should be comparing notes about what they see as the needs and wants of the market, and planning ways to improve the offering of services to meet those needs.

Strategic planning may have historically been the exclusive domain of business types. Physicians looking to integrate may even be looking to gain the benefits of strategic planning from the business types. But I think strategic planning for the future of healthcare must come from a partnership of thinking, from a merging of minds. Clinicians and executives working together will have a significant advantage over competitors who fail to communicate at a high and successful level. Strategic planning cannot be relegated to a department or to those with primary interest in the discipline. It must be a shared responsibility to capture the best perspectives of both physicians and managers.

MAINTAINING ECONOMIC SOUNDNESS

The ultimate test of a successful acquisition is found in its ability to maintain and develop economic soundness over an extended period of time. Financial stability is a solid indicator of balanced interests, common understanding about the goals of the integrated organization, and mutual respect of the key players. The converse is also true. Financial instability is frequently a sign of unbalanced interests, confusion, and disrespect.

The primary purpose of this book has been to prevent financial instability in medical practice acquisitions. As we have seen, sound business relationships are possible if they are based on sound business principles. Those principles include fair valuation, using the techniques and concepts described in the earlier chapters. They include win–win negotiations following the model in Chapter 6. They require full disclosure and honest communication. The principles of fair dealing extend beyond the transaction to include successfully blending unlike corporate cultures and responding strategically to changes in the market.

The fundamental changes impacting healthcare will likely continue to fuel the interest in developing integrated systems. The stellar performers in that new environment will be those who learn to work together in long-term win–win relationships. I hope that you will be a part of that future, helped in some way by the sound business principles you learned in this book.

11
CHAPTER

Medical
Practice Mergers

The effects of medical competition are causing physicians to look for help both vertically, with hospitals, and horizontally, with other physicians. Medical groups has been one of the fastest growing segments of the healthcare industry. In 1969, the American Medical Association reported just over 6,000 groups, comprising of 40,000 physicians, operating in the United States. By 1995, over 16,000 groups with more than 180,000 physicians were active, and the size of the groups was found to be growing faster than the number of groups. The Medical Group Management Association, organized in 1923 to serve the needs of nonphysician medical group executives, more than doubled in size between 1985 and 1995.[1]

As a result of the growth in medical groups, physicians now have additional options if they seek to join the main-

1. The Medical Group Management Associaiton (MGMA) has excellent resources for anyone active in managing physician services. They can be reached at 104 Inverness Terrace East, Englewood, CO 80112–5306. 303-799-1111.

stream of managed care. Mergers of two or more groups are becoming viable alternatives for physicians in many communities, and the dynamics of forming new organizations are, for some, a less daunting option than selling out.

MERGER VERSUS ACQUISITION

Merging is buying and selling under another name. It involves two or more parties coming together into a new organization to benefit each other, a lot like a hospital buying a medical practice. But mergers are different in certain ways, and those differences can impact the appraisal process.

Similarities to Buying and Selling

Medical mergers are similar to acquisitions in several ways, and the principles outlined in this book relative to acquisitions apply directly in these areas.

Role of the Appraisal   Merging organizations can benefit from an appraisal in the same way buyers and sellers can benefit from an acquisition appraisal. The nature of the appraisal is quite different, but the need for mutual discovery and documentation of assets is just as important, if not more so, in a merger. The nature and mechanics of a merger appraisal are addressed later in this chapter.

Negotiation   The skills of the negotiators are likely to have a direct impact on the outcome of a merger. Since the parties are on a more equal footing than in the case of a hospital acquisition of a medical practice, the negotiation process can be pivotal. And mutual trust is a cornerstone of fair and equitable negotiations, just as it is in acquisitions.

Governance   Merged organizations need structures for decision making, as do vertically integrated health systems.

The governance structure is likely to be quite different than it would appear if the practice is part of a division of the hospital, but both kinds of organizations need to have a way of getting things done.

Tax Issues   Mergers have tax consequences for both parties, just as acquisitions do. The tax issues may be different, and they may be centered on particular segments of the transaction such as how to deal with the retirement plan, but they will need to be dealt with under the advice of qualified professionals.

Dissimilar Issues

Mergers will also require different treatment of some of the same issues raised in medical practice acquisitions. Understanding the differences can help the parties determine the feasibility of the merger, and its relevance to the market.

Physician to Physician   The nature of a merger is considerably different because of the position of the parties. Unlike an acquisition of a medical practice by an institution, a merger puts physicians across the bargaining table with physicians. Sometimes it even places former competitors in a potentially cooperative posture with each other. There is more likely to be greater equality in understanding the business dynamics than there is in an acquisition involving physicians and seasoned business executives. A merger is more like the friendly inclusion of a new partner to an existing group practice.

Business Risk   Mergers generally keep both parties at risk for business success. When an institution acquires a practice, the bulk of business risk typically shifts to the hospital, but physicians in a merged organization are still fully subject to the risks and rewards of business ownership. That risk may be shared, but it is still there.

Emphasis on Relative Contributions   The appraisal and negotiation processes are more likely to focus on the relative contributions of each party than to measure with precision the specific goodwill value each brings to the bargaining table. Likewise, an emphasis on income distribution methods will become the focal point of compensation negotiations, rather than dwelling on base salaries and benefits.

Relevance to the Market   Mergers are a horizontal marketing strategy rather than a vertical marketing strategy. Physicians considering a merger will have to discern whether joining with other physicians separate from a hospital will be a more successful strategy in the long term, or whether they will be better off linked to an inpatient institution. Both strategies can be relevant to the demands of the market. The local circumstances will have to be interpreted to draw wise business conclusions, but the difference between the two strategies should be fully understood.

New Issues

Mergers also pose issues that are not generally part of the discussion in acquisitions.

Antitrust   In some communities, mega-mergers of medical groups may raise concerns about monopolistic control of the market. Those issues are present in relatively few hospital acquisitions of practices, but they may become larger issues as groups grow in size relative to their communities.

Compensation   If the merged organization includes physicians from different specialties, compensation issues are likely to emerge at center stage. Merging the interests of specialists with the interests of primary care physicians can test the mettle of any seasoned executive. Those complexities are likely to grow as capitation-based managed care contracts increase. There are no perfect formulas, but by keeping a focus on the reasons for staying together in a group, physicians and their administrators can usually find creative solutions to the compensation dilemma.

MECHANICS OF MERGER APPRAISALS

The appraisal process for a merger focuses less on specific measurements of tangible and intangible value, and more on the relative contributions of each party. The objective of an appraisal in a merger is to make sure the interests of the parties are balanced, and to have a plan for dealing with imbalances. The desired balance of interests comes by negotiating the relative values of both tangible and intangible assets.

Tangible Assets

The first step in conducting an appraisal for a proposed merger is to prepare, and then combine, economic balance sheets for the merger partners. The process is detailed in Chapter 2, and it involves restating the assets and liabilities after adjusting for items such as accounts receivable at market value, liabilities that will not be assumed by the merged organization, and similar items.

Furniture and equipment should be appraised at fair market value, according to their age and condition. If an independent appraiser is engaged to conduct the valuation of equipment, the same appraiser should be used for each party to the merger, yielding a consistent valuation.

Accounts receivable are more likely to be transferred to the new organization in a merger than they would be if a hospital were to acquire the practice. The cash flows will be necessary to finance operations, and the businesses are similar enough to make the merger of accounts relatively seamless.

A merger appraisal should also take unstated liabilities into consideration, such as accrued vacation and sick leave for support staff. These benefits are more likely to be rolled over into the merged organization than they would be if the practice was acquired by a new organization with established policies and protocols.

Physicians' vehicles can represent a potentially sticky negotiating point in a merger. If one practice has a tradition of including physicians' vehicles in the practice assets, perhaps with related car loans, and the other does not, the appraisal and negotiation process will need to resolve the difference in traditions. A simple solution is to transfer ownership of the practice-owned vehicles to their physicians simultaneously with the merger transaction.

Intangible Assets

A merger appraisal may look quite different from its acquisition counterpart when it comes to measuring intangible values. I recommend focusing on the relative contributions of the factors of production, including the following components:

> Gross charges
> Net receipts
> Relative value units
> Medical records
> Visit volume
> Payer mix
> Management and staff
> Information systems

Let's take a closer look at each of these components.

Gross Charges   The first measure of goodwill is the relative contribution to overall gross charges. Higher producers will contribute more to the economic strength of the merged organization, whether their production advantage comes from their specialty and procedural capabilities, or from their hard-working practice patterns. If the fee schedules of the merger partners are widely variant on common codes, the relative contributions of gross charges might be skewed.

Net Receipts Net receipts offer a more sensitive measure of relative effort than gross charges, particularly when fees are widely variant. This is a measure of the money that went into the bank, and it is therefore a solid measure of relative economic significance.

Relative Value Units Converting the procedural codes and volumes to relative value units at each practice is another refinement in the measurement of relative contributions that may be easier in some practices than it is in others. If the practice has an existing computer system that automates the conversion to the Resource Based Relative Value System designed for the Medicare system, the process is simple. If conversions are required manually, the refinement may not be workable.

Medical Records One of the most valuable segments of the intangible assets is symbolized by the medical records. The records represent patients who are likely to return regularly for medical care, fueling the financial stability of the merged organization. The active records are obviously more valuable than inactive ones, so a common definition of an active record is essential. In my experience, defining active records as those records of patients seen at least once in the past three years seems most appropriate. Coincidentally, most medical practices seem to have just enough shelf space for three years of records. Inactive records may have more limited value. Their value is evident only if they represent new business through reactivation.

Visit Volume In the fee-for-service environment, volume is a key factor in productivity. Those physicians who work extended hours and who manage their time efficiently produce at higher levels, and their relative contribution to the merger will be more extensive. In the capitated contract environment, visit volume measurements may need to be supplemented with documentation of covered lives or member months. The more covered lives a partner contributes to the merger, the greater that partner's contribution.

Payer Mix   The reimbursement patterns of each merger partner will depend heavily on the payer mix of her patient base. Physicians with limited Medicare and Medicaid patient bases will contribute more to the economic partnership than those faced with extensive contractual discounts. Measuring the impact of the payer mix may be less intuitive than measuring medical records or patient visits, and the reimbursement results may be impacted by factors other than those controlled by the payer mix. I recommend assigning a value from 1 to 10 for the overall impact of the payer mix for each merger partner, and measuring the relative contribution of those assigned values.

Management and Staff   Two factors are essential to consider with this component of productivity. The number of staff relative to physicians is a measure of the overhead efficiency of each practice, and the competence of each staff member is a contributor to his long-term value to the merged organization. Measuring the former is easy; the latter requires subjective judgment. Determine the ratio of full-time equivalent support staff to full-time equivalent physicians at each practice by counting normalized weekly labor hours and dividing by 40 hours. The lower the staff ratio, the more efficient the practice. Measuring the relative competence of each staff member might be best accomplished through negotiation by the physicians that know their work best.

Information Systems   In most merger situations, the merged organization will need to invest in a larger, more current information system. But in some circumstances, one of the merger partners may have the foundation for an information system that can be expanded to meet the needs of the

EXHIBIT 11-1

Example of Merger Appraisal Worksheet

	Practice A	Practice B	Practice C	Total
FTE Providers	2.0	3.0	3.5	
Gross Charges	$396,545	$662,715	$1,016,706	$2,075,966
Percent	19%	32%	49%	100%
Receipts	$375,000	$440,843	$887,811	$1,703,654
Percent	22%	26%	52%	100%
Active Medical Records	6,800	6,500	12,000	25,300
Percent	27%	26%	47%	100%
Equipment Inventories at Market Value	$51,649	$73,470	$103,915	$229,034
Percent	23%	32%	45%	100%
Average of Percents	**23%**	**29%**	**48%**	

larger, growing group. If the foundation has value, the relative contribution of that value should accrue to its owners.

Once the measurements of each factor of productivity have been obtained, the relative contribution of each practice to each factor can be measured as a percent of the whole, factor by factor. Then calculating a simple average of the percentages yields a final estimate of the relative contribution each party is making to the goodwill value.

CONCLUSION

Merging medical practices is usually less complex than structuring an outright acquisition, and the historical record seems to demonstrate their greater likelihood of success. The rapid growth of medical groups, and their increasing size, is a testament to the profitability and market relevance of medical group practice. It stands in contrast to the recent pattern of losses in the hospital-owned medical practice market. But the long-term viability of horizontal integration strategies versus vertically integrated organizations remains to be seen.

APPENDIX

Revenue Ruling 59–60

Edited, with emphasis added

In valuing the stock of closely held corporations, or the stock of corporations where market quotations are not available, all other available financial data, as well as all relevant factors affecting the fair market value, must be considered for estate tax and gift tax purposes. **No general formula may be given that is applicable to the many different valuation situations** arising in the valuations of such stock. However, the general approach, methods, and factors that must be considered in valuing such securities are outlined.

SECTION I. PURPOSE

The purpose of this Revenue Ruling is to outline and review in general the approach, methods, and factors to be considered in valuing shares of the capital stock of closely held corporations for estate tax and gift tax purposes. The methods discussed herein will apply likewise to the valuation of corporate stocks on which market quotations are either unavailable or are of such scarcity that they do not reflect the fair market value.

SECTION 2. BACKGROUND AND DEFINITIONS

.01 All valuations must be made in accordance with the applicable provisions of the Internal Revenue Code of 1954 and the Federal Estate Tax and Gift Tax Regulations. Sections 2031 (a) and 2512 (a) of the 1954 Code require that the property to be included in the gross estate, or made the subject of a gift, shall be taxed on the basis of the value of the property at the time of death of the decedent, the alternate date if so elected, or the date of gift.

.02 Section 20.2031–1 (b) of the Estate Tax Regulations (section 81.10 of the Estate Tax Regulations 105) and section 25.2512–1 of the Gift Tax Regulations (section 86.19 of Gift Tax Regulations 108) define **fair market value**, in effect, as **the price at which the property would change hands between a willing buyer and a willing seller when the former is not under any compulsion to buy and the latter is not under any compulsion to sell, both parties having reasonable knowledge of relevant facts. Court decisions frequently state in addition that the hypothetical buyer and seller are assumed to be able, as well as willing, to trade and to be well informed about the property and concerning the market for such property.**

.03 Closely held corporations are those corporations the shares of which are owned by a relatively limited number of stockholders. Often the entire stock issue is held by one family. The result of this situation is that little, if any, trading in the shares takes place. There is, therefore, no established market for the stock and such sales as occur at irregular intervals seldom reflect all of the elements of a representative transaction, as defined by the term "fair market value."

SECTION 3. APPROACH TO VALUATION

.01 A determination of fair market value, being a question of fact, will depend upon the circumstances in each case. **No formula can be devised that will be generally applicable** to the multitude of different valuation issues arising in estate and gift tax cases. Often, an appraiser will find wide differences of opinion as to the fair market value of a particular stock. In resolving such differences, he should maintain a reasonable attitude in recognition of the fact that valuation is not an exact science. **A sound valuation will be based upon all the relevant facts, but the elements of common sense, informed judgment, and reasonableness must enter into the process** of weighing those facts and determining their aggregate significance.

.02 The fair market value of specific shares of stock will vary as general economic conditions change from "normal" to "boom" or "depression," that is, according to the degree of optimism or pessimism with which the investing public regards the future at the required date of appraisal. Uncertainty as to the stability or continuity of the future income from a property decreases its value by increasing the risk of loss of earnings and value in the future. The value of shares of stock of a company with very uncertain future prospects is highly speculative. The appraiser must exercise his judgment as to the degree of risk attaching to the business of the corporation that issued the stock, but that judgment must be related to all of the other factors affecting value.

.03 **Valuation** of securities is, in essence, **a prophecy as to the future** and must be based on facts available at the required date of appraisal. As a generalization, the prices of stocks which are traded in volume in a free and active market by informed persons best reflect the consensus of the investing public as to what the future holds for the corporations and industries represented. When a stock is closely held, is traded infrequently, or is traded in an erratic market, some other measure of value must be used. In many instances, the next best measure may be found in the prices at which the stocks of companies engaged in the same or a similar line of business are selling in a free and open market.

SECTION 4. FACTORS TO CONSIDER

.01 It is advisable to emphasize that in the valuation of the stock of closely held corporations or the stock of corporations where market quotations are either lacking or too scarce to be recognized, all available financial data, as well as all relevant factors affecting the fair market value, should be considered. **The following factors,** although not all-inclusive, **are fundamental and require careful analysis in each case:**

  (a) The nature of the business and the history of the enterprise from its inception.

  (b) The economic outlook in general and the condition and outlook of the specific industry in particular.

  (c) The book value of the stock and the financial condition of the business.

  (d) The earning capacity of the company.

  (e) The dividend-paying capacity.

  (f) Whether or not the enterprise has goodwill or other intangible value.

  (g) Sales of the stock and the size of the block or stock to be valued.

  (h) The market price of stocks of corporations engaged in the same or a similar line of business shaving their stocks actively traded in a free and open market, either on an exchange or over-the-counter.

.02 The following is a brief discussion of each of the foregoing factors:

  (a) The history of a corporate enterprise will show its past stability or instability, its growth or lack of growth, the diversity or lack of diversity of its operations, and other facts needed to form an opinion of the degree of risk involved in the business. For an enterprise that changed its form of organization but carried on the same or closely similar operations of its predecessor, the history of the former enterprise should be considered. The detail to be considered should increase with approach to the required date of appraisal, since recent events are of greatest help in predicting the future; but a study of gross and net income, and of dividends covering a long prior period, is highly desirable. The history to be studied should include, but need not be limited to, the nature of the business, its products or services, its operating and investment assets, capital structure, plant facilities, sales records and management, all of which should be considered as of the date of the appraisal, with due regard for recent significant changes. Events of the past that are unlikely to recur in the future should be discounted, since value has a close relation to future expectancy.

(b) A sound appraisal of a closely held stock must consider current and prospective economic conditions as of the date of appraisal, both in the national economy and in the industry or industries with which the corporation is allied. It is important to know that the company is more or less successful than its competitors in the same industry, or that it is maintaining a stable position with respect to competitors. Equal or even greater significance may attach to the ability of the industry with which the company is allied to compete with other industries. Prospective competition, which has not been a factor in prior years, should be given careful attention. For example, high profits due to the novelty of its prospect and the lack of competition often lead to increasing competition. The public's appraisal of the future products of competitive industries or of competitors within an industry may be indicated by price trends in the markets for commodities and for securities. The loss of the manager of a so-called "one-man" business may have a depressing effect upon the value of the stock of such business, particularly if there is a lack of trained personnel capable of succeeding to the management of the enterprise. In valuing the stock of this type of business, therefore, the effect of the loss of the manager on the future expectancy of the business, and the absence of management-succession potentialities are pertinent factors to be taken into consideration. On the other hand, there may be factors which offset, in whole or in part, the loss of the manager's services. For instance, the nature of the business and of its assets may be such that they will not be impaired by the loss of the manager. Furthermore, the loss may be adequately covered by life insurance, or competent management might be employed on the basis of the consideration paid for the former manager's services. These, or other offsetting factors, if found to exist, should be carefully weighed against the loss of the manager's services in valuing the stock of the enterprise.

(c) Balance sheets should be obtained, preferably in the form of comparative annual statements for two or more years immediately preceding the date of appraisal, together with a balance sheet at the end of the month preceding that date, if corporate accounting will permit. Any balance sheet descriptions that are not self-explanatory, and balance sheet items comprehending diverse assets or liabilities, should be clarified in essential detail by supporting supplemental schedules. These statements usually will disclose to the appraiser (1) liquid position (ratio of current assets to current liabilities); (2) gross and net book value of principal classes of fixed assets; (3) working capital; (4) long-term indebtedness; (5) capital structure; and (6) net worth. Consideration also should be given to any assets not essential to the operation of the business, such as investments in securities, real estate, etc. In general, such nonoperating assets will command a lower rate of return than do the operating assets, although in exceptional cases the reverse may be true. **In computing the book value per share of stock, assets of the investment type should be revalued on the basis of their**

market price and the book value adjusted accordingly. Comparison of the company's balance sheets over several years may reveal, among other facts, such developments as the acquisition of additional production facilities or subsidiary companies, improvement in financial position, and details as to recapitalizations and other changes in the capital structure of the corporation. If the corporation has more than one class of stock outstanding, the charter or certificate of incorporation should be examined to ascertain the explicit rights and privileges of the various stock issues, including: (1) voting powers, (2) preference as to dividends, and (3) preference as to assets in the event of liquidation.

(d) **Detailed profit-and-loss statements should be obtained and considered for a representative period** immediately prior to the required date of appraisal, **preferably five or more years.** Such statements should show (1) gross income by principal items; (2) principal deductions from gross income, including major prior items of operating expenses, interest and other expense on each item of long-term debt, depreciation and depletion if such deductions are made, officers' salaries, in total if they appear to be reasonable or in detail if they seem to be excessive, contributions (whether or not deductible for tax purposes) that the nature of its business and its community position require the corporation to make, and taxes by principal items, including income and excess profits taxes; (3) net income available for dividends; (4) rates and amounts of dividends paid on each class of stock; (5) remaining amount carried to surplus; and (6) adjustments to, and reconciliation with, surplus as stated on the balance sheet. With profit and loss statements of this character available, the appraiser should be able to separate recurrent from nonrecurrent items of income and expense, to distinguish between operating income and investment income, and to ascertain whether or not any line of business in which the company is engaged is operated consistently at a loss and might be abandoned with benefit to the company. The percentage of earnings retained for business expansion should be noted when dividend-paying capacity is considered. **Potential future income is a major factor in many valuations of closely held stocks,** and all information concerning past income that will be helpful in predicting the future should be secured. Prior earnings records usually are the most reliable guide as to the future expectancy, but **resorting to arbitrary 5- or 10-year averages without regard to current trends or future prospects will not produce a realistic valuation.** If, for instance, a record of progressively increasing or decreasing net income is found, then greater weight may be accorded the most recent years' profits in estimating earning power. It will be helpful, in judging risk and the extent to which a business is a marginal operation, to consider deductions from income and net income in terms of percentage of sales. Major categories of cost and expense to be so analyzed include the consumption of raw materials and supplies in the case of manufacturers, processors, and fabricators; the cost of purchased merchandise in the case of merchants; utility services; insurance; taxes; depletion or depreciation; and interest.

(e) Primary consideration should be given to the dividend-paying capacity of the company rather than to dividends actually paid in the past. Recognition must be given to the necessity of retaining a reasonable portion of profits in a company to meet competition. Dividend-paying capacity is a factor that must be considered in an appraisal, but dividends actually paid in the past may not have any relation to dividend-paying capacity. Specifically, **the dividends paid by a closely held family company may be measured by the income needs of the stockholders or by their desire to avoid taxes on dividend receipts, instead of by the ability of the company to pay dividends. Where an actual or effective controlling interest in a corporation is to be valued, the dividend factor is not a material element,** since the payment of such dividends is discretionary with the controlling stockholders. The individual or group in control can substitute salaries and bonuses for dividends, thus reducing net income and understating the dividend-paying capacity of the company. It follows, therefore, that **dividends are less reliable criteria of fair market value than other applicable factors.**

(f) In the final analysis, goodwill is based upon earning capacity. The presence of goodwill and its value, therefore, rests upon the excess of net earnings over and above a fair return on the net tangible assets. While the element of goodwill may be based primarily on earnings, such factors as the prestige and renown of the business, the ownership of a trade or brand name, and a record of successful operation over a prolonged period in a particular locality, also may furnish support for the inclusion of intangible value. In some instances it may not be possible to make a separate appraisal of the tangible and intangible assets of the business. The enterprise has a value as an entity. Whatever intangible value there is, which is supportable by the facts, may be measured by the amount by which the appraised value of the tangible assets exceeds the net book value of such assets.

(g) Sales of stock of a closely held corporation should be carefully investigated to determine whether they represent transactions at arm's length. Forced or distress sales do not ordinarily reflect fair market value nor do isolated sales in small amounts necessarily control as the measure of value. This is especially true in the valuation of a controlling interest in a corporation. Since, in the case of closely held stocks, no prevailing market prices are available, there is no basis for making an adjustment for blockage. It follows, therefore, that such stocks should be valued upon a consideration of all the evidence affecting the fair market value. The size of the block of stock itself is a relevant factor to be considered. Although it is true that a minority interest in an unlisted corporation's stock is more difficult to sell than a similar block of listed stock, it is equally true that control of a corporation, either actual or in effect, representing as it does an added element of value, may justify a higher value for a specific block of stock.

(h) Section 2031 (b) of the Code states, in effect, that **in valuing unlisted securities the value of stock or securities of corporations engaged in the same or a similar line of business which are listed on an exchange should be taken into consideration along with all other factors.** An important consideration is that the corporations to be used for comparisons have capital stocks that are actively traded by the public. In accordance with section 2031 (b) of the Code, stocks listed on an exchange are to be considered first. However, if sufficient comparable companies whose stocks are listed on an exchange cannot be found, other comparable companies that have stocks actively traded in on the over-the-counter market also may be used. The essential factor is that whether the stocks are sold on an exchange or over-the-counter there is evidence of an active, free public market for the stock as of the valuation date. **In selecting corporations for comparative purposes, care should be taken to use only comparable companies.** Although the only restrictive requirement as to comparable corporations specified in the statute is that their lines of business be the same or similar, yet it is obvious that consideration must be given to other relevant factors in order that the most valid comparison possible will be obtained. For illustration, a corporation having one or more issues of preferred stock, bonds, or debentures in addition to its common stock should not be considered to be directly comparable to one having only common stock outstanding. In like manner, a company with a declining business and decreasing markets is not comparable to one with a record of current progress and market expansion.

SECTION 5. WEIGHT TO BE ACCORDED VARIOUS FACTORS

The valuation of closely held corporate stock entails the consideration of all relevant factors as stated in Section 4. Depending upon the circumstances in each case, certain factors may carry more weight than others because of the nature of the company's business. To illustrate:

  (a) Earnings may be the most important criterion of value in some cases, whereas asset value will receive primary consideration in others. In general, the appraiser will accord primary consideration to earnings when valuing stocks of companies that sell products or services to the public; conversely, in the investment or holding type of company, the appraiser may accord the greatest weight to the assets underlying the security to be valued.

  (b) The value of the stock of a closely held investment or real estate holding company, whether or not family owned, is closely related to the value of the assets underlying the stock. For companies of this type the appraiser should determine the fair market values of the assets of the company. Operating expenses of such a company and the cost of liquidating it, if any, merit consideration when appraising the relative values of the stock and the underlying assets. The market values of the underlying assets give due weight to potential earnings and dividends of the particular items of property underlying the stock, capitalized at rates deemed proper by the investing public at the date of appraisal. A current appraisal by the investing public should be superior to the retrospective opinion of an individual. For these reasons, adjusted net worth should be accorded greater weight in valuing the stock of a closely held investment or real estate holding company, whether or not family owned, than any of the other customary yardsticks of appraisal, such as earnings and dividend paying capacity.

SECTION 6. CAPITALIZATION RATES

In the application of certain fundamental valuation factors, such as earnings and dividends, it is necessary to capitalize the average or current results at some appropriate rate. **A determination of the proper capitalization rate presents one of the most difficult problems in valuation.** That there is no ready or simple solution will become apparent by a cursory check of the rates of return and dividend yields in terms of the selling prices of corporate shares listed on the major exchanges of the country. Wide variations will be found even for companies in the same industry. Moreover, the ratio will fluctuate from year to year depending upon economic conditions. Thus, **no standard tables of capitalization rates applicable to closely held corporations can be formulated.** Among the more important factors to be taken into consideration in deciding upon a capitalization rate in a particular case are: (1) the nature of the business; (2) the risk involved; and (3) the stability or irregularity of earnings.

SECTION 7. AVERAGE OF FACTORS

Because valuations cannot be made on the basis of a prescribed formula, **there is no means whereby the various applicable factors in a particular case can be assigned mathematical weights in deriving the fair market value.** For this reason, no useful purpose is served by taking an average of several factors (for example, book value, capitalized earnings, and capitalized dividends) and basing the valuation on the result. Such a process excludes active consideration of other pertinent factors, and the end result cannot be supported by a realistic application of the significant facts in the case except by mere chance.

SECTION 8. RESTRICTIVE AGREEMENTS

Frequently, in the valuation of closely held stock for estate and gift tax purposes, it will be found that the stock is subject to an agreement restricting its sale or transfer. Where shares of stock were acquired by a decedent subject to an option reserved by the issuing corporation to repurchase at a certain price, the option is usually accepted as the fair market value for estate tax purposes. However, in such case the option price is not determinative of fair market value for gift tax purposes. Where the option, or buy and sell agreement, is the result of voluntary action by the stockholders, such agreement may or may not, depending upon the circumstance of each, fix the value for estate tax purposes. However, such agreement is a factor to be considered, with other relevant factors, in determining fair market value. Where the stockholder is free to dispose of his shares during life and the option is to become effective only upon his death, the fair market value is not limited to the option price. It is always necessary to consider the relationship of the parties, the relative number of shares held by the decedent, and other material facts, to determine whether the agreement represents a bona fide business arrangement or is a device to pass the decedent's share to the natural objects of his bounty for less than an adequate and full consideration in money or money's worth.

B

Revenue Ruling 68–609

Edited, with emphasis added

The "formula" approach may be used in determining the fair market value of intangible assets of a business only if there is no *better* **basis** available for making the determination.

The purpose of this Revenue Ruling is to update and restate, under the current statute and regulations, the currently outstanding portions of A.R.M. 34, C.B. 2, 31 (1920), A.R.M. 68, C.B. 3, 43 (1920), and O.D. 937, C.B. 4, 43, (1921).

The question presented is whether the "formula" approach, the capitalization of earnings in excess of a fair rate of return on net tangible assets, may be used to determine the fair market value of the intangible assets of a business.

The **"formula" approach may be stated as follows:**

A percentage return on the average annual value of the tangible assets used in a business is determined, using a period of years (preferably not less than five) immediately prior to the valuation date. **The amount of the percentage return on tangible assets,**

thus determined **is deducted from the average earnings of the business for such period and the remainder, if any, is considered to be the amount of the average annual earnings from the intangible assets of the business** for the period. **This amount** (considered as the average annual earnings from intangibles), **capitalized** at a percentage of say, 15 to 20 percent, **is the value of the intangible assets of the business determined under the "formula" approach.**

The percentage of return on the average annual value of the tangible assets used should be the percentage prevailing in the industry involved at the date of valuation, or (when the industry percentage is not available) a percentage of 8 to 10 percent may be used.

The 8 percent rate of return and the 15 percent rate of capitalization are applied to tangibles and intangibles, respectively, of businesses with a small risk factor and stable and regular earnings, the 10 percent rate of return and 20 percent rate of capitalization are applied to businesses in which the hazards of business are relatively high.

The above rates are used as examples and are not appropriate in all cases. In applying the "formula" approach, **the average earnings period and the capitalization rates are dependent upon the facts** pertinent thereto **in each case.**

The past earnings to which the formula is applied should fairly reflect the probable future earnings. Ordinarily, the period should not be less than five years, and abnormal years, whether above or below the average, should be eliminated. **If the business is a sole proprietorship or partnership, there should be deducted from the earnings of the business a reasonable amount for services performed by the owner or partners engaged in the business.** See *Lloyd B. Sanderson Estate v. Commissioner,* 42 F. 2d 160 (1830). Further, only the tangible assets entering into net worth, including accounts and bills receivable in excess of accounts and bills payable, are used for determining earnings on the tangible assets. **Factors that influence the capitalization rate include (1) the nature of the business, (2) the risk involved, and (3) the stability or irregularity of earnings.**

The "formula" approach should not be used if there is **better** evidence available from which the value of intangibles can be determined. **If the assets of a going business are sold upon the basis of a rate of capitalization that can be substantiated as being realistic, though it is not within the range of figures indicated here as the ones ordinarily to be adopted, the same rate of capitalization should be used in determining the value of intangibles.**

Accordingly, the **"formula" approach may be used for determining the fair market value of intangible assets of a business only if there is no** *better* basis therefore available.

See also Revenue Ruling 59–60, C.B. 1959–1, 237, as modified by Revenue Ruling 65–193, C.B. 1965–2, 370, which sets forth the proper approach to use in the valuation of closely held corporate stocks for estate and gift tax purposes. The general approach, methods, and factors, outlined in Revenue Ruling 59–60, as modified, are equally applicable to valuations of corporate stocks for income and other tax purposes as well as for estate and gift tax purposes. They apply also to problems involving the determination of the fair market value of business interests of any type, including partnerships and proprietorship, and of intangible assets for all tax purposes.

C

Present Value Tables

Present Value of One Dollar Due at the End of n Periods

$$PV = \frac{\$1}{r} - \frac{\$1}{r(1+r)^n}$$

PV = present value; r = discount rate; n = number of periods payment is made.

n	1%	2%	3%	4%	5%	6%	7%	8%	9%	10%	n
1	.99010	.98039	.97007	.96154	.95238	.94340	.93458	.92593	.91743	.90909	1
2	.98030	.96117	.94260	.92456	.90703	.89000	.87344	.85734	.84168	.82645	2
3	.97059	.94232	.91514	.88900	.86384	.83962	.81630	.79383	.77218	.75131	3
4	.96098	.92385	.88849	.85480	.82270	.79209	.76290	.73503	.70843	.68301	4
5	.95147	.90573	.86261	.82193	.78353	.74726	.71299	.68058	.64993	.62092	5
6	.94204	.88797	.83748	.79031	.74622	.70496	.66634	.63017	.59627	.56447	6
7	.93272	.87056	.81309	.75992	.71068	.66506	.62275	.58349	.54703	.51316	7
8	.92348	.85349	.78941	.73069	.67684	.62741	.58201	.54027	.50187	.46651	8
9	.91434	.83675	.76642	.70259	.64461	.59190	.54393	.50025	.46043	.42410	9
10	.90529	.82035	.74409	.67556	.61391	.55839	.50835	.46319	.42241	.38554	10
11	.89632	.80426	.72242	.64958	.58468	.52679	.47509	.42888	.38753	.35049	11
12	.88745	.78849	.70138	.62460	.55684	.49697	.44401	.39711	.35553	.31863	12
13	.87866	.77303	.68095	.60057	.53032	.46884	.41496	.36770	.32618	.28966	13
14	.86996	.75787	.66112	.57747	.50507	.44230	.38782	.34046	.29925	.26333	14
15	.86135	.74301	.64186	.55526	.48102	.41726	.36245	.31524	.27454	.23939	15
16	.85282	.72845	.62317	.53391	.45811	.39365	.33873	.29189	.25187	.21763	16
17	.84438	.71416	.60502	.51337	.43630	.37136	.31657	.27027	.23107	.19784	17
18	.83602	.70016	.58739	.49363	.41552	.35034	.29586	.25025	.21199	.17986	18
19	.82774	.68643	.57029	.47464	.39573	.33051	.27651	.23171	.19449	.16351	19
20	.81954	.67297	.55367	.45639	.37689	.31180	.25842	.21455	.17843	.14864	20
21	.81143	.65978	.53755	.43883	.35894	.29415	.24151	.19866	.16370	.13513	21
22	.80340	.64684	.52189	.42195	.34185	.27750	.22571	.18394	.15018	.12285	22
23	.79544	.63414	.50669	.40573	.32557	.26180	.21095	.17031	.13778	.11168	23
24	.78757	.62172	.49193	.39012	.31007	.24698	.19715	.15770	.12640	.10153	24
25	.77977	.60953	.47760	.37512	.29530	.23300	.18425	.14602	.11597	.09230	25

Present Value of One Dollar Due at the End of *n* Periods

n	11%	12%	13%	14%	15%	16%	17%	18%	19%	20%	n
1	.90090	.89286	.88496	.87719	.86957	.86207	.85470	.84746	.84034	.83333	1
2	.81162	.79719	.78315	.76947	.75614	.74316	.73051	.71818	.70616	.69444	2
3	.73119	.71178	.69305	.67497	.65752	.64066	.62437	.60863	.59342	.57870	3
4	.65873	.63552	.61332	.59208	.57175	.55229	.53365	.51579	.49867	.48225	4
5	.59345	.56743	.54276	.51937	.49718	.47611	.45611	.43711	.41905	.40188	5
6	.53464	.50663	.48032	.45559	.43233	.41044	.38984	.37043	.35214	.33490	6
7	.48166	.45235	.42506	.39964	.37594	.35383	.33320	.31392	.29592	.27908	7
8	.43393	.40388	.37616	.35056	.32690	.30503	.28478	.26604	.24867	.23257	8
9	.39092	.36061	.33288	.30751	.28426	.26295	.24340	.22546	.20897	.19381	9
10	.35218	.32197	.29459	.26974	.24718	.22668	.20804	.19106	.17560	.16151	10
11	.31728	.28748	.26070	.23662	.21494	.19542	.17781	.16192	.14756	.13459	11
12	.28584	.25667	.23071	.20756	.18691	.16846	.15197	.13722	.12400	.11216	12
13	.25751	.22917	.20416	.18207	.16253	.14523	.12989	.11629	.10420	.09346	13
14	.23199	.20462	.18068	.15971	.14133	.12520	.11102	.09855	.08757	.07789	14
15	.20900	.18270	.15989	.14010	.12289	.10793	.09489	.08352	.07359	.06491	15
16	.18829	.16312	.14150	.12289	.10686	.09304	.08110	.07078	.06184	.05409	16
17	.16963	.14564	.12522	.10780	.09293	.08021	.06932	.05998	.05196	.04507	17
18	.15282	.13004	.11081	.09456	.08080	.06914	.05925	.05083	.04367	.03756	18
19	.13768	.11611	.09806	.08295	.07026	.05961	.05064	.04308	.03669	.03130	19
20	.12403	.10367	.08678	.07276	.06110	.05139	.04328	.03651	.03084	.02608	20
21	.11174	.09256	.07680	.06383	.05313	.04430	.03699	.03094	.02591	.02174	21
22	.10067	.08264	.06796	.05599	.04620	.03819	.03162	.02622	.02178	.01811	22
23	.09069	.07379	.06014	.04911	.04017	.03292	.02702	.02222	.01830	.01509	23
24	.08170	.06588	.05322	.04308	.03493	.02838	.02310	.01883	.01538	.01258	24
25	.07361	.05882	.04710	.03779	.03038	.02447	.01974	.01596	.01292	.01048	25

Present Value of One Dollar Due at the End of n Periods

n	21%	22%	23%	24%	25%	26%	27%	28%	29%	30%	n
1	.82645	.81967	.81301	.80645	.80000	.79365	.78740	.78125	.77519	.76923	1
2	.68301	.67186	.66098	.65036	.64000	.62988	.62000	.61035	.60093	.59172	2
3	.56447	.55071	.53738	.52449	.51200	.49991	.48819	.47684	.46583	.45517	3
4	.46651	.45140	.43690	.42297	.40960	.39675	.38440	.37253	.36111	.35013	4
5	.38554	.37000	.35520	.34111	.32768	.31488	.30268	.29104	.27993	.26933	5
6	.31863	.30328	.28878	.27509	.26214	.24991	.23833	.22737	.21700	.20718	6
7	.26333	.24859	.23478	.22184	.20972	.19834	.18766	.17764	.16822	.15937	7
8	.21763	.20376	.19088	.17891	.16777	.15741	.14776	.13878	.13040	.12259	8
9	.17986	.16702	.15519	.14428	.13422	.12493	.11635	.10842	.10109	.09430	9
10	.14864	.13690	.12617	.11635	.10737	.09915	.09161	.08470	.07836	.07254	10
11	.12285	.11221	.10258	.09383	.08590	.07869	.07214	.06617	.06075	.05580	11
12	.10153	.09198	.08339	.07567	.06872	.06245	.05680	.05170	.04709	.04292	12
13	.08391	.07539	.06780	.06103	.05498	.04957	.04472	.04039	.03650	.03302	13
14	.06934	.06180	.05512	.04921	.04398	.03934	.03522	.03155	.02830	.02540	14
15	.05731	.05065	.04481	.03969	.03518	.03122	.02773	.02465	.02194	.01954	15
16	.04736	.04152	.03643	.03201	.02815	.02478	.02183	.01926	.01700	.01503	16
17	.03914	.03403	.02962	.02581	.02252	.01967	.01719	.01505	.01318	.01156	17
18	.03235	.02789	.02408	.02082	.01801	.01561	.01354	.01175	.01022	.00889	18
19	.02673	.02286	.01958	.01679	.01441	.01239	.01066	.00918	.00792	.00684	19
20	.02209	.01874	.01592	.01354	.01153	.00983	.00839	.00717	.00614	.00526	20
21	.01826	.01536	.01294	.01092	.00922	.00780	.00661	.00561	.00476	.00405	21
22	.01509	.01259	.01052	.00880	.00738	.00619	.00520	.00438	.00369	.00311	22
23	.01247	.01032	.00855	.00710	.00590	.00491	.00410	.00342	.00286	.00239	23
24	.01031	.00846	.00695	.00573	.00472	.00390	.00323	.00267	.00222	.00184	24
25	.00852	.00693	.00565	.00462	.00378	.00310	.00254	.00209	.00172	.00142	25

Present Value of an Annuity of One Dollar for n Periods

$$PV = \frac{\$1}{r}(1+r)^n$$

PV = present value; r = discount rate; n = number of periods until payment.

n	1%	2%	3%	4%	5%	6%	7%	8%	9%	10%	n
1	.9901	.9804	.9709	.9615	.9524	.9434	.9346	.9259	.9174	.9091	1
2	1.9704	1.9416	1.9135	1.8861	1.8594	1.8334	1.8080	1.7833	1.7591	1.7355	2
3	2.9410	2.8839	2.8286	2.7751	2.7232	2.6730	2.6243	2.5771	2.5313	2.4868	3
4	3.9020	3.8077	3.7171	3.6299	3.5459	3.4651	3.3872	3.3121	3.2397	3.1699	4
5	4.8535	4.7134	4.5797	4.4518	4.3295	4.2123	4.1002	3.9927	3.8896	3.7908	5
6	5.7955	5.6014	5.4172	5.2421	5.0757	4.9173	4.7665	4.6229	4.4859	4.3553	6
7	6.7282	6.4720	6.2302	6.0020	5.7863	5.5824	5.3893	5.2064	5.0329	4.8684	7
8	7.6517	7.3254	7.0196	6.7327	6.4632	6.2098	5.9713	5.7466	5.5348	5.3349	8
9	8.5661	8.1622	7.7861	7.4353	7.1078	6.8017	6.5152	6.2469	5.9852	5.7590	9
10	9.4714	8.9825	8.5302	8.1109	7.7217	7.3601	7.0236	6.7101	6.4176	6.1446	10
11	10.3677	9.7868	9.2526	8.7604	8.3064	7.8868	7.4987	7.1389	6.8052	6.4951	11
12	11.2552	10.5753	9.9539	9.3850	8.8632	8.3838	7.9427	7.5361	7.1607	6.8137	12
13	12.1338	11.3483	10.6349	9.9856	9.3935	8.8527	8.3576	7.9038	7.4869	7.1034	13
14	13.0038	12.1062	11.2960	10.5631	9.8986	9.2950	8.7454	8.2442	7.7861	7.3667	14
15	13.8651	12.8492	11.9379	11.1183	10.3796	9.7122	9.1079	8.5595	8.0607	7.6061	15
16	14.7180	13.5777	12.5610	11.6522	10.8377	10.1059	9.4466	8.8514	8.3125	7.8237	16
17	15.5624	14.2918	13.1660	12.1656	11.2740	10.4772	9.7632	9.1216	8.5436	8.0215	17
18	16.3984	14.9920	13.7534	12.6592	11.6895	10.8276	10.0591	9.3719	8.7556	8.2014	18
19	17.2261	15.6784	14.3237	13.1339	12.0853	11.1581	10.3356	9.6036	8.9501	8.3649	19
20	18.0457	16.3514	14.8774	13.5903	12.4622	11.4699	10.5940	9.8181	9.1285	8.5136	20
21	18.8571	17.0111	15.4149	14.0291	12.8211	11.7640	10.8355	10.0168	9.2922	8.6487	21
22	19.6605	17.6580	15.9368	14.4511	13.1630	12.0416	11.0612	10.2007	9.4424	8.7715	22
23	20.4559	18.2921	16.4435	14.8568	13.4885	12.3033	11.2722	10.3710	9.5802	8.8832	23
24	21.2435	18.9139	16.9355	15.2469	13.7986	12.5503	11.4693	10.5287	9.7066	8.9847	24
25	22.0233	19.5234	17.4131	15.6220	14.0939	12.7833	11.6536	10.6748	9.8226	9.0770	25

Present Value of an Annuity of One Dollar for *n* Periods

n	11%	12%	13%	14%	15%	16%	17%	18%	19%	20%	n
1	.9009	.8929	.8850	.3772	.8696	.8621	.8547	.8475	.8403	.8333	1
2	1.7125	1.6901	1.6681	1.6467	1.6257	1.6052	1.5852	1.5656	1.5465	1.5278	2
3	2.4437	2.4018	2.3612	2.3216	2.2832	2.2459	2.2096	2.1743	2.1399	2.1065	3
4	3.1024	3.0373	2.9745	2.9137	2.8550	2.7982	2.7432	2.6901	2.6386	2.5887	4
5	3.6959	3.6048	3.5172	3.4331	3.3522	3.2743	3.1993	3.1272	3.0576	2.9906	5
6	4.2305	4.1114	3.9976	3.8887	3.7845	3.6847	3.5892	3.4976	3.4098	3.3255	6
7	4.7122	3.5638	4.4226	4.2883	4.1604	4.0386	3.9224	3.8115	3.7057	3.6046	7
8	5.1461	4.9676	4.7988	4.6389	4.4873	4.3436	4.2072	4.0776	3.9544	3.8372	8
9	5.5370	5.3282	5.1317	4.9464	4.7716	4.6065	4.4506	4.3030	4.1633	4.0310	9
10	5.8892	5.6502	5.4262	5.2161	5.0188	4.8332	4.6586	4.4941	4.3389	4.1925	10
11	6.2065	5.9377	5.6869	5.4527	5.2337	5.0286	4.8364	4.6560	4.4865	4.3271	11
12	6.4924	6.1944	5.9176	5.6603	5.4206	5.1971	4.9884	4.7932	4.6105	4.4392	12
13	6.7499	6.4235	6.1218	5.8424	5.5831	5.3423	5.1183	4.9095	4.7147	4.5327	13
14	6.9819	6.6282	6.3025	6.0021	5.7245	5.4675	5.2293	5.0081	4.8023	4.6106	14
15	7.1909	6.8109	6.4624	6.1422	5.8474	5.5755	5.3242	5.0916	4.8759	4.6755	15
16	7.3792	6.9740	6.6039	6.2651	5.9542	5.6685	5.4053	5.1624	4.9377	4.7296	16
17	7.5488	7.1196	6.7291	6.3729	6.0472	5.7487	5.4746	5.2223	4.9897	4.7746	17
18	7.7016	7.2497	6.8399	6.4674	6.1280	5.8178	5.5339	5.2732	5.0333	4.8122	18
19	7.8393	7.3658	6.9380	6.5504	6.1982	5.8775	5.5845	5.3162	5.0700	4.8435	19
20	7.9633	7.4694	7.0248	6.6231	6.2593	5.9288	5.6278	5.3527	5.1009	4.8696	20
21	8.0751	7.5620	7.1016	6.6870	6.3125	5.9731	5.6648	5.3837	5.1268	4.8913	21
22	8.1757	7.6446	7.1695	6.7429	6.3587	6.0113	5.6964	5.4099	5.1486	4.9094	22
23	8.2664	7.7184	7.2297	6.7921	6.3988	6.0442	5.7234	5.4321	5.1668	4.9245	23
24	8.3481	7.7843	7.2829	6.8351	6.4338	6.0726	5.7465	5.4509	5.1822	4.9371	24
25	8.4217	7.8431	7.3300	6.8729	6.4641	6.0971	5.7662	5.4669	5.1951	4.9476	25

Present Value of an Annuity of One Dollar for n Periods

n	21%	22%	23%	24%	25%	26%	27%	28%	29%	30%	n
1	.8264	.8197	.8130	.8065	.8000	.7937	.7874	.7813	.7752	.7692	1
2	1.5095	1.4915	1.4740	1.4568	1.4400	1.4235	1.4074	1.3916	1.3761	1.3609	2
3	2.0739	2.0422	2.0114	1.9813	1.9520	1.9234	1.8956	1.8684	1.8420	1.8161	3
4	2.5404	2.4936	2.4483	2.4043	2.3616	2.3202	2.2800	2.2410	2.2031	2.1662	4
5	2.9260	2.8636	2.8035	2.7454	2.6893	2.6351	2.5827	2.5320	2.4830	2.4356	5
6	3.2446	3.1669	3.0923	3.0205	2.9514	2.8850	2.8210	2.7594	2.7000	2.6427	6
7	3.5079	3.4155	3.3270	3.2423	3.1611	3.0833	3.0087	2.9370	2.8682	2.8021	7
8	3.7256	3.6193	3.5179	3.4212	3.3289	3.2407	3.1564	3.0758	2.9986	2.9247	8
9	3.9054	3.7863	3.6731	3.5655	3.4631	3.3657	3.2728	3.1842	3.0997	3.0190	9
10	4.0541	3.9232	3.7993	3.6819	3.5705	3.4648	3.3644	3.2689	3.1781	3.0915	10
11	4.1769	4.0354	3.9018	3.7757	3.6564	3.5435	3.4365	3.3351	3.2388	3.1473	11
12	4.2785	4.1274	3.9852	3.8514	3.7251	3.6060	3.4933	3.3868	3.2859	3.1903	12
13	4.3624	4.2028	4.0530	3.9124	3.7801	3.6555	3.5381	3.4272	3.3224	3.2233	13
14	4.4317	4.2646	4.1082	3.9616	3.8241	3.6949	3.5733	3.4587	3.3507	3.2487	14
15	4.4890	4.3152	4.1530	4.0013	3.8593	3.7261	3.6010	3.4834	3.3726	3.2682	15
16	4.5364	4.3567	4.1894	4.0333	3.8874	3.7509	3.6228	3.5026	3.3896	3.2832	16
17	4.5755	4.3908	4.2190	4.0591	3.9099	3.7705	3.6400	3.5177	3.4028	3.2948	17
18	4.6079	4.4187	4.2431	4.0799	3.9279	3.7861	3.6536	3.5294	3.4130	3.3037	18
19	4.6346	4.4415	4.2627	4.0967	3.9424	3.7985	3.6642	3.5386	3.4210	3.3105	19
20	4.6567	4.4603	4.2786	4.1103	3.9539	3.8083	3.6726	3.5458	3.4271	3.3158	20
21	4.6750	4.4756	4.2916	4.1212	3.9631	3.8161	3.6792	3.5514	3.4319	3.3198	21
22	4.6900	4.4882	4.3021	4.1300	3.9705	3.8223	3.6844	3.5558	3.4356	3.3230	22
23	4.7025	4.4985	4.3106	4.1371	3.9764	3.8273	3.6885	3.5592	3.4384	3.3254	23
24	4.7128	4.5070	4.3176	4.1428	3.9811	3.8312	3.6918	3.5619	3.4406	3.3272	24
25	4.7213	4.5139	4.3232	4.1474	3.9849	3.8342	3.6943	3.5640	3.4423	3.3286	25

D

A P P E N D I X

Internal Medicine Associates, P.C.

Practice Appraisal
June 1994

The following case study offers a demonstration of format and technique. It is fictional, although the information used and the approach followed are similar to the circumstances found in many practices and many appraisals. Its similarity to any particular practice is purely coincidental.

Description of the Assignment

Hutton Hospital requested an appraisal of the tangible and intangible assets of Internal Medicine Associates, P.C., to set the stage for negotiation of the sale of the practice. The professional corporation operates a group medical practice, while a subsidiary, Internal Medical Leasing Company, holds both the office condominium real estate and the equipment used by Internal Medicine Associates, P.C. The value of the real estate is determined contractually, and is not within the scope of this appraisal. This appraisal examines the tangible and intangible assets of the practice as of May 31, 1994.

The most commonly used definition of fair market value is located in Revenue Ruling 59–60. This revenue ruling defines fair market value as

> the price at which the property would change hands between a willing buyer and a willing seller when the former is not under any compulsion to buy and the latter is not under any compulsion to sell, both parties having reasonable knowledge of relevant facts.

Description of the Property

The scope of this appraisal is to measure the fair market value of the tangible assets of cash, accounts receivable, and equipment, and the intangible assets of the employees, the patient relationships, and the value of the practice as a going concern. We will approach this appraisal as though all assets and liabilities are part of one entity, even though the final transaction will involve a separation of equipment values from the remainder of the practice.

Limiting Conditions

The data gathered for the analyses of value were drawn from the financial statements, billing records, medical records, and from personal observations of the appraiser at the time of the site visit. Fee schedules were produced by the support staff of the practice, and information regarding the professional intentions of the physicians were drawn from interviews with each of the six physician stockholders and two employed physicians.

Appraisal Methods

Method # 1 is the Net Asset Value method, which is a restatement of book value after an examination of the collectible value of the accounts receivable, an appraisal of the equipment on the basis of its remaining useful life, and a calculation of the present value of projected future debts to which the practice is already obligated.

Method # 2 is a Capitalization approach based on IRS Revenue Ruling 68-609 to develop the value of intangible assets, modified to be more appropriate for medical practices.

Method # 3 is the Guideline Comparison Method. We compare the circumstances of Internal Medicine Associates, P.C., with those of similar medical practices sold throughout the United States, as reported in the *Goodwill Registry* produced by The Health Care Group of Plymouth Meeting, Pennsylvania.

Method # 4 reflects the Replacement Value of the company. This method combines facts and perspectives on both the tangible and intangible value of the medical practice.

The results of all four methods are then weighted, using the professional judgment of the appraiser, to yield a final conclusion of value.

Appraiser's Disinterest

The appraiser hereby declares that he has no present or contemplated future interest in the subject property or any other interest that might tend to prevent his making a fair and unbiased appraisal.

VALUATION CALCULATIONS

Method #1: Net Asset Value

The first method calls for a restatement of book value after an examination of the collectible value of the accounts receivable, an appraisal of the equipment on the basis of its remaining useful life, and a calculation of the present value of projected debts incurred by the repurchase of stock from Drs. Steth and Syringe. The net asset value of tangible assets will be combined with goodwill estimates from the other appraisal methods to yield estimates of total value.

Accounts receivable are charges owed by patients and their insurers to Internal Medicine Associates, P.C. They are booked at the standard fees, regardless of how they will be paid by the insurer. Medicare, Medicaid, HMOs and other insurers frequently disallow a portion of the charge, resulting in a write-off of the uncollectible portion. In 1993, the company was able to recognize as income about 77 percent of its gross charges before contractual write-offs, and 98 percent of its gross charges after contractual write-offs. Income was recognized on the cash basis. Our objective with this part of the appraisal is to estimate the collectible value of the accounts receivable.

The accounts receivable has been relatively steady in the past year. Based on the most recent statement (May 31, 1994), the accounts receivable can be valued to yield the following projections of cash:

Age	Book Value	Collectibility	Estimated Cash Value
0–30 days	$112,007	90%	$100,806
30–60 days	$76,844	80%	$61,475
60–90 days	$48,050	60%	$28,830
90–120 days	$29,392	40%	$11,757
120 days +	$50,426	20%	$10,085
unbilled	$100,001	90%	$90,000
Total	$417,221		$302,953

The second component of this appraisal method is to establish the value of the equipment owned by Internal Medicine Associates, P.C., and Internal Medical Leasing. We conducted a physical inventory of all equipment and supplies on May 31, 1994, and estimated the market value on the basis of replacement costs and the remaining useful life of each item. The total value of equipment at useful life is appraised at $128,200, and the practice maintains about two months of office, clinical, and lab supplies valued at about $45,400. A detailed list of the equipment and its market value is included in the addendum to this report.

The third component in this appraisal method is to estimate the present value of future expected debts. The most significant debt included in this analysis is the remaining commitment to the buyout of Dr. Steth, which occured in 1993, and the projected buyout of Dr. Syringe, anticipated on June 30, 1994. The remaining commitments are valued exclusive of the agreements concerning Dr. Steth's respective shares of the real estate. Approximately $19,000 is still owed to Dr. Steth, which is part of the long-term debt identified on the balance sheet of March 31, 1994. The final value owed to Dr. Syringe under the terms of his employment agreement with Internal Medicine Associates, P.C., are not able to be determined precisely until after June 30, 1994, but our projection of the value of his stock and accounts receivable at that point is that they will total $45,000.

With these three pieces, we can now restate the May 31, 1994, balance sheet as follows:

Assets	At Book	At Market
Accounts Receivable	$417,221	$303,000
Equipment (from Internal Medical Leasing)	$169,000	$128,200
Cash and Prepaids (as of 3/31/96)	$65,500	$65,500
Supplies	$0	$45,500
TOTAL ASSETS	$651,721	$542,200
Liabilities		
Current Liabilities	$17,500	$17,500
Long-term Liabilities (from P.C.)	$101,300	$101,300
Long-term Liabilities (from Leasing)	$121,000	$121,000
Present Value of Dr. Syringe's buyout	$0	$45,000
TOTAL LIABILITIES	$239,800	$284,800
Equity or Net Asset Value	*$411,921*	*$257,400*
Total Liabilities and Equity	*$651,721*	*$542,200*

Method #2: Capitalization of Normalized Earnings

Normalized Earnings

To gain a clear understanding of the cash flows that may be transferrable and discretionary to the new owners, we focused on normalized excess earnings. Excess earnings is defined as the physician compensation earned beyond the median for the specialty, according to national data. Adjustments were also made for abnormal cash flows and for transactions that benefit the current owners and that are not expected to be transferred. In the case of IMA, compensation reflects salaries, bonuses, and dividend income from the leasing company. Normalized income is calculated as the arithmetic mean of the past five years. Since we are only capitalizing the excess earnings, which represent, the intangible assets, the result of this method will need to be added to the net asset value of tangible assets to yield a complete view of total value.

This is how the analysis looks for Internal Medicine Associates, P.C.:

Excess Earnings per IMA Shareholder 1989–1993

	1989	1990	1991	1992	1993
Number of Shareholders	4	6	6	6	6
Avg. Shareholder Comp.	$147,318	$142,948	$144,936	$148,572	$126,592
Median IM Earnings	$103,990	$110,606	$112,722	$119,538	$125,000
Excess Earnings per Physician	$43,328	$32,342	$32,214	$29,034	$1,592
Excess Earnings Totals	$173,312	$194,052	$193,284	$174,204	$9,552

Normalized Excess Earnings, Five Year Mean   **$148,881**

Note: Median IM earnings are drawn from consecutive *Physician Compensation and Production Surveys* from the Medical Group Management Association for the years 1989 through 1993.

It is important to note that the excess earnings dropped precipitously in 1993. To the extent that this earnings decline is a reflection of market forces, the future potential for excess earnings might be seriously endangered. In our view, it would be unfair to value the goodwill simply on the basis of historical patterns without a clear plan for repeating that history under changing market conditions. This factor will be re-considered when we weigh the results of each method.

Development of the Capitalization Rate

Section 6 of Revenue Ruling 59–60 states:

> "In the application of certain fundamental valuation factors, such as earnings and dividends, it is necessary to capitalize the average or current results at some appropriate rate. A determination of the proper capitalization rate presents one of the most difficult problems in valuation."

In the text of Revenue Ruling 69–608, capitalization rates of 15 percent to 20 percent were mentioned as an example. Many appraisers are under the misconception that the capitalization rate must stay within this range. In reality, the capitalization rate must be consistent with the rate of return currently needed to attract capital to the type of investment in question.

There are various methods of determining capitalization rates. Using the built-up method of determining a capitalization rate results in a rate as follows:

TABLE 2

Capitalization Rate Buildup

"Safe" rate (a)	7.50%
General Risk Premium (b)	7.30%
Small Company Risk Premium (c)	5.10%
Specific Company Risk Premium (d)	2.00%
SUBTOTAL	21.90%
Capitalization Rate (rounded)	22%

Notes for Table 2:

(a) *The Wall Street Journal*, 10-year Treasury Bonds, May 31, 1994.

(b) *Stocks, Bonds, Bills and Inflation 1992 Yearbook,* Ibbotson Associates, difference between total return on common stocks and long-term government bonds from 1926 to 1992.

(c) *Stocks, Bonds, Bills and Inflation 1993 Yearbook,* Ibbotson Associates, difference between total return on small company stocks and common stocks from 1926 to 1992.

(d) See next section on development of the specific company risk premium.

Developing the Specific Company Risk Premium

Determining the risk associated with a specific medical practice requires extensive professional judgment by an independent evaluator familiar with the details of operating a medical practice. We profiled the practice and compared its performance on several key productivity indicators to offer an informed opinion of the business risks faced and the relative achievements of the three physicians. The measurements of performance are drawn from the data analyzed at the time of the site visit. The standards for comparison are drawn from data assembled by the Medical Group Management Association, publications by *Medical Economics* and the American Medical Association, and from our experience as medical management consultants and appraisers to dozens of similar practices. The risk factors are derived from our proprietary database of appraisals.

TABLE 3

Key Indicators of Business Risk/Success

Indicator	Standard	IMA	Risk Factor
Overhead as percent of net receipts	50%	60%	–5%
Net receipts per physician	$360,000	$420,000	+5%
Annual volume of office visits per physician	4,600	4,500	0%
Average age of accounts receivable in days	75	90	–2%
Volume of active charts per physician	2,000	2,200	+4%
Total Risk Value			+2%

To complete the capitalization of normalized earnings, we divide the normalized earning by the capitalization rate as follows:

$$\frac{\$148,881}{22\%} = \$676,732$$

Adding the net asset value to the capitalized normalized earnings produces a conclusion of value.

Capitalization of normalized excess earnings	$676,732
Net asset value at fair market value	$257,400
Total Value (rounded)	**$934,000**

Method # 3: Guideline Comparison Method

The Health Care Group of Plymouth Meeting, Pennsylvania, has conducted a continuous survey of healthcare consultants involved in the appraisal of medical practices since 1985. The data is updated annually, showing the goodwill values determined in a large variety of specialties, in urban and rural settings, and under various sales conditions. The *1994 Goodwill Registry* reports the goodwill as a percent of annual practice receipts, with the cumulative median since 1985 for internal medicine practices at just under 27 percent. Thirty practices out of the 208 transactions reported in this period were conducted with no value for goodwill. The best values were awarded to the practices with the lowest overhead.

A comparison of the specific factors of value, using the *Goodwill Registry*, does not yield a clear conclusion of the goodwill value for IMA. The risk factors considered in the capitalization build-up technique demonstrate that the practice is fairly comparable to the norm for internal medicine practices nationwide. Their strong experience in net receipts and volume of active charts is compromised by their high overhead and collection difficulties, yielding a net result that is only slightly above average for their peers. Our conclusion, then, is that if the guideline comparison method has any contribution to make to our understanding of goodwill value in this case, it should be applied using the average of 27 percent of net receipts.

If the 27 percent value were applied to 1993 receipts of $2,370,000 for IMA, the goodwill value would be estimated at approximately $640,000.

Adding the net asset value to the results of the guideline comparisons method produces a conclusion of value:

Guideline comparisons conclusion of value	$640,000
Net asset value at fair market value	$257,400
Total Value (rounded)	**$897,000**

Method #4: The Replacement Value Method

The intangible assets, collectively referred to as "goodwill," include the characteristics that make Internal Medicine Associates, P.C., a going concern. "Goodwill" is a term derived from accounting, designed to categorize an amount received for the purchase of stock in excess of book value. It is recorded on the corporate books after the transaction and it is a reflection of the negotiated settlement after the fact. The overall purpose in valuing goodwill is to try to answer the question, What would it take to replicate the organization in its current form if we started from nothing? How much would it cost to replace equipment with new and used furnishings? How much would the owners have to defer in earnings to develop the cash flow the organization now enjoys?

This method calls for the greatest professional judgment, and is therefore subject to the widest variation in concluding values. Its primary purpose is to examine the assumptions about the value of the components of intangible assets, and as such it is helpful in contributing to an understanding of stock values when combined with other methods. Tangible and intangible values are rounded for convenience.

Internal Medicine Associates, P.C., Replacement Value Method

Estimated Costs to Replace:

Furniture, fixtures, and equipment	$200,000
Recruitment for eight midcareer internists	$200,000
Operating capital	$150,000
Operating losses until practice maturity	$400,000
Total Replacement Costs	**$950,000**

Supporting Assumptions for the Replacement Value Method

Furniture, Fixtures, and Equipment: This represents the cost of new furniture, fixtures, and equipment comparable in volume and quantity to the current holdings of the practice and its leasing company. The actual cost may vary if either the amount of furniture or the style of replacement items were to change.

Recruitment of Eight Midcareer Internists: The recruitment costs are estimated at $25,000 each, which is the appraiser's estimate of a typical finder's fee in the current market for general internists.

Operating Capital: The cash requirements for operations are estimated to be approximately three weeks' cash flow, based on the previous year's net receipts.

Operating Losses Until Practice Maturity: The most volatile component of the replacement cost method is the estimate of operating losses a start-up practice of similar size and specialty might face. The figure offered in this analysis is considered by the appraiser to be a conservative value of $50,000 per physician, estimated to be incurred in the first two years of a start-up. The estimate can vary according to the competition, management skill, physician incentives, and payer mix faced by the new practice.

WEIGHTING OF METHODS

The results of the first method yielded an estimate of net asset value at fair market value, which is carried forward into methods two and three. The results of methods two, three, and four are as follows:

Capitalization of Normalized Excess Earnings plus NAV	$934,000
Guideline Comparisons plus NAV	$897,000
Replacement Value Method	$950,000

In the appraiser's judgment, each method has weaknesses and strengths. The capitalization method examines excess earnings, which may or may not be transferrable to the purchaser, depending on the decisions buyers and sellers make regarding employment and incentive structures. The drop in earnings of the past year can serve as an argument that future benefits to practice ownership may be compromised. The guideline comparison method does not offer specific comparisons to similar practices in the same geographic market and the same time period. The national trend for internal medicine practices over the past decade may or may not be an adequate guideline for comparison. The replacement estimates can vary widely, particularly in examining the projected losses to maturity. The volatility of the replacement method weakens its conclusions in a similar manner as the weakness of other methods.

These limitations seem to be relatively equal, however, which draws us to conclude that the final determination of value should be based on an equal weighting of the three valuation estimates.

The weighting is applied as follows:

Method	Estimate	Weight	Weighted Value
Capitalization Method	$934,000	33.3%	$311,333
Guideline Comparisons	$897,000	33.3%	$299,133
Replacement Value Method	$950,000	33.3%	$316,667
Net Valuation (rounded)			$927,000

Certification

I hereby certify that, to the best of my knowledge and belief, the statements of fact contained in this report are true and correct, and this report has been prepared in conformity with the Uniform Standards of Professional Appraisal Practice of the Appraisal Foundation and the Principles of Appraisal Practice and Code of Ethics of the American Society of Appraisers.

The Appraisal Firm

E

John Freewilly, M.D., P.C.
Practice Appraisal
March 1996

The following case study offers a demonstration of format and technique. It is fictional, although the information used and the approach followed are similar to the circumstances found in many practices and many appraisals. Its similarity to any particular practice is purely coincidental.

Description of the Assignment

Caring Hospital has expressed their interest in acquiring the medical practice assets of Dr. John Freewilly, and employing Dr. Freewilly and his brother, Dr. Tom Freewilly. Appraisal Associates, Inc., was engaged to appraise the tangible and intangible value of the practice at fair market value as of March 7, 1996.

The most commonly used definition of fair market value is located in Revenue Ruling 59–60. This revenue ruling defines fair market values as

. . . the price at which the property would change hands
between a willing buyer and a willing seller when the former is not under any compulsion to buy and the latter is
not under any compulsion to sell, both parties having reasonable knowledge of relevant facts.

Description of the Property

The scope of this appraisal is to measure the fair market
value of the tangible assets of cash, accounts receivable, and
equipment, and the intangible assets of the practice as a
going concern. In Dr. Freewilly's case, some of the tangible
assets (most of the medical and office equipment) are held
outside the corporation as personal assets. We will approach
this appraisal as though all assets and liabilities are part of
one entity, even though the final transaction may involve a
separation of equipment values from the remainder of the
practice. Dr. Freewilly also owns the medical office building
in which his practice is located, but the valuation of real estate is beyond the scope of this appraisal and is therefore
excluded from the conclusion of value.

The practice is fully owned by Dr. John Freewilly, although he practices with a limited schedule. His brother,
Dr. Tom Freewilly, works a very full schedule as an employed physician in the practice. Dr. John Freewilly limits
his office schedule because of health concerns to three half-
days per week, 36 weeks per year. Dr. Tom Freewilly
works approximately four full days in the office each week,
49 weeks per year. Together they comprise the equivalent
of approximately 1.3 FTE physicians, and are projected to
provide approximately 6,500 office visits in 1996. The
practice maintains about 2,700 active charts, according to
the estimate developed by a count of a sample of the actual
charts. The practice reported their estimate of 4,000 active
charts. An active chart is defined as the record of a patient
who has been seen at least once in the past two years.

The practice has been in operation in the Caring area
for 17 years. It has been refined to meet the unique needs

of both physicians, and to build upon their respective interests. Dr. John Freewilly indicated that he enjoys a limited patient schedule, devoting the rest of his time to developing management strategies for the practice and to personal leisure. He is officially disabled and collects personal income from a disability insurance policy. His status requires him to limit his structured compensation from the practice to not exceed $21,000 annually. Additional compensation is earned by leasing the furniture and equipment to the practice at the rate of $1,000 per month, leasing the building to the practice at the rate of $5,000 per month, incurring automobile expense through the practice worth about $1,000 per month, and enjoying perks like significant continuing medical education trips. The practice is carefully structured to enhance Dr. John Freewilly's role as the owner and manager, which he enjoys.

Dr. Tom Freewilly was characterized by his brother as a diligent and hard-working physician who loves to concentrate on patient care without the hassle of management responsibility. Dr. Tom Freewilly's compensation includes operating profits for the business, as though he were the owner. His diligence is demonstrated by his volume of office visits, estimated at approximately 4,800 in 1995. He is the most voluminous admitter to Caring Hospital, which is located adjacent to the practice. In 1995, he accounted for 244 admissions, according to data from the hospital president.

The payer mix at the practice is estimated from an analysis of the accounts receivable to be:

Medicare	44%
BCBS	23%
Commercial	16%
HMO 1	10%
HMO 2	5%
Medicaid	2%

The practice employs four support staff who work schedules that equate to 3.5 full-time equivalents. Billing is conducted with an in-house computer system that is operated on technologically obsolete equipment. Despite the noncurrent resources, the practice has historically maintained its accounts receivable at an average age of approximately 60 days. An aggressive discount for payment at the time of service has helped keep the collection process relatively uncomplicated.

The facilities consist of five exam rooms in addition to the waiting room, reception area, office manager's area, and physician's office. There is no X-ray facility, and the practice performs only waived tests in its limited lab area. The facilities also have five other exam rooms that are used periodically by a visiting physician. The area used by the Freewillys is estimated to be approximately 2,500 square feet.

Limiting Conditions

The data gathered for the analyses of value were drawn from the financial statements, billing records, medical records, and from personal observations of the appraiser at the time of the site visit. Fee schedules were produced by the support staff of the practice, and information regarding the professional intentions of the two physicians were drawn from interviews with Dr. John Freewilly.

The financial statements reviewed were prepared without audit by Professional CPAs, Inc. The unique patterns of compensating Dr. John Freewilly with benefits other than income is partially documented in the financial statements, such that comparing the expenses to other benchmark practices requires extensive assumptions.

Sources of Information

The following sources of information were used for this appraisal:

1. Unaudited income statements for the practice for the 12-month periods ending May 1993, May 1994,

and May 1995. We also examined the balance sheet dated January 31, 1996, and the income statement for the eight moths ending January 1996.

2. U.S. Corporation Income Tax Returns (Form 1120) for fiscal years ending May 31, 1994, and May 31, 1995.

3. The professional fee schedule in use as of March 1996.

4. The aged accounts receivable by payer type as of March 7, 1996.

5. A tabulation of office visits by physician per half-day for the months of September and November 1995.

6. Inventory of equipment, furniture, and medical records conducted by the appraiser on site on March 7, 1996.

7. *Cost Survey,* Medical Group Management Association, 1995.

8. *Physician Production and Compensation Survey,* Medical Group Management Association, 1995.

9. *Goodwill Registry,* The Health Care Group, 1995.

10. *The 1995 Physician Practice Acquisition Resource Book,* The Center for Healthcare Industry Performance Standards, 1995.

11. Conversations with Dr. John Freewilly.

Appraisal Methods

Method # 1 is Net Asset Value (NAV) method, which is a restatement of book value after an examination of the collectible value of the accounts receivable, an appraisal of the equipment on the basis of its remaining useful life, and after other adjustments.

Method # 2 is the Excess Earnings Plus NAV method. The excess earnings method is an income-based approach that seeks to measure the value of goodwill as evidenced by exceptional profitability. The results of the analysis are added to the net asset value of tangible assets to yield the total value.

Method # 3 estimates the replacement value of the company. This method combines facts and perspectives on both the tangible and intangible value of the medical practice.

The results of all the methods are then weighted, using the professional judgment of the appraiser, to yield a final conclusion of value. That value is then tested by comparing it to data from other similar practice acquisitions.

Appraiser's Disinterest

The appraiser hereby declares that he has no present or contemplated future interest in the subject property or any other interest that might tend to prevent his making a fair and unbiased appraisal.

VALUATION CALCULATIONS

Method #1: Net Asset Value

The net asset value approach to appraising calls for a restatement of the book value of the corporation at fair market value. The book value frequently excludes certain assets such as accounts receivable, and may contain assets or liabilities that are not expected to be acquired by the buyer. The most recent balance sheet constructed for the practice is dated January 31, 1996.

JOHN FREEWILLY, M.D., P.C.
Balance Sheet
January 31, 1996

Current Assets			
Checking		$17,479	
Accounts Receivable		$10,703	
Total Current Assets			$28,182
Fixed Assets			
Furniture and Equipment	$32,024		
Less Depreciation	$28,306	$3,718	
Computer Software	$4,000		
Less Depreciation	–$3,970	$30	
Total Fixed Assets			$3,748
Total Assets			$31,930
Liabilities			
State Tax Withheld		–$99	
Federal Tax Withheld		–$133	
Account Payable, Tom Freewilly, M.D.		$1,132	
Total Liabilities			$901
Equity			
Common Stock			$3,124
Retained Earnings		$3,089	
Net Gain		$24,817	
Total Retained Earnings			$27,906
Total Equity			$31,030
Total Liabilities and Equity			$31,930

The following observations about the book value are important to note for the purposes of the appraisal:

1. Cash is unlikely to be part of the acquisition if a transaction takes place, so its economic value to a potential buyer will be zero. Also, the total retained earnings will most likely be distributed to the shareholder prior to the acquisition, so they are excluded from the value. Finally, the billing software is not likely to be acquired since it is inconsistent with the hospital's system.

2. Accounts receivable was found from internal records to be quite different from the value shown on the balance sheet. The accounts receivable as of March 7, 1996, were found to have a book value of $52,871. Based on their age and payer mix, the collectible value is estimated to be $31,555.

3. The furniture, fixtures, and equipment are held partly by the corporation and partly by Dr. John Freewilly. The portion he holds personally is leased back to the corporation, although the lease agreement is undocumented. For the purposes of the appraisal, all furniture, fixtures, and equipment were inventoried and appraised at fair market value on March 7, 1996. The total fair market value was determined to be $44,020. The detail is included in the appendix.

With these three pieces, we can now restate the March 7, 1996, balance sheet as follows:

Assets	At Book	At Market
Cash	$17,479	$0
Accounts Receivable	$10,479	$31,555
Equipment	$3,748	$44,020
Total Assets	$31,930	$75,575
Liabilities		
Liabilities	$901	$901
Equity or Net Asset Value	$31,030	$74,674
Total Liabilities and Equity	$31,930	$75,575

Method #2: Excess Earnings Plus NAV

Excess Earnings

To gain a clear understanding of the cash flows that may be transferrable and discretionary to the new owners, we focused on normalized excess earnings. Excess earnings is defined as the physician compensation earned beyond the median for the specialty, according to national data. Adjustments were also made for abnormal cash flows and for transactions that benefit the current owners that may or may not be transferrable. In the case of Dr. Freewilly's practice, compensation reflects salaries, bonuses, automobiles, medical reimbursement, and earned income from leasing the building, furniture, and equipment to the practice. Further adjustments are required to estimate the full-time equivalency of the two physicians. Normalized income is calculated as the arithmetic mean of the past three years.

The estimated excess earnings are then capitalized at a rate estimated to be sufficient to attract capital investment, given the business risk associated with owning and operating the medical practice. The capitalization rate is developed on the basis of several components of risk, and based on research of risk rates in other medical practices. Since we are only capitalizing the excess earnings, which represents the intangible assets, the result of this method will need to be added to the net asset value of tangible assets to yield a complete view of total value.

This is how the analysis looks for John Freewilly, M.D., P.C.:

Income Analysis
Fiscal Years 1993–1995

	1993	1994	1995
Receipts	$382,390	$381,118	$421,376
Expenses			
Staff wages and salaries	$48,284	$48,921	$71,560
Supplies	21,066	19,796	33,191
Telephone	8,889	8,243	7,185
Accounting and legal fees	14,881	8,655	6,840
Insurance	8,360	14,489	16,342
Total CME	13,684	9,526	15,796
Other overhead expense	37,298	34,356	23,026
Total Overhead Expense	$152,462	$143,986	$173,940
Profit			
Tom Freewilly, M.D.			
Wages	$113,500	$121,000	$125,000
Auto	6,997	10,655	8,592
Total Tom Freewilly	$120,497	$131,655	$133,592
John Freewilly, M.D.			
Wages	$18,500	$21,000	$21,000
Auto	14,706	10,488	12,504
Medical reimbursement	12,070	10,131	8,402
Equipment lease revenue	12,253	13,372	13,008
Rent revenue	50,708	55,000	55,128
Total John Freewilly	$108,237	$109,951	$110,042
Net Income (Loss)	$1,194	($4,474)	$3,802

The relative stability of revenue and profits of the past three years may not be indicative of the future revenue stream for the practice. Dr. John Freewilly adjusted his schedule in January 1996 to take more time off than he has in previous years. The accounts receivable was reported to be fairly stable at about $100,000 in the past several years, but we found it to be at about $53,000 on March 7, 1996, which is an indication that the cash flow is declining as Dr. Freewilly takes more time away from the practice.

Our best estimate about the full-time equivalency of the physicians for the period 1993 through 1995 is based on discussions with Dr. John Freewilly. We estimate that the two physicians functioned during this time as the equivalency of 1.5 physicians, although the projection is that in 1996 they will function at the 1.3 FTE level.

It should be noted that we left the full value of continuing education in overhead expenses, and did not segregate the market value of rent on the equipment and building from the excess value received by Dr. John Freewilly. The analysis is not pure, but it is a good reflection of true cash flows that benefit the physicians directly.

To estimate the excess earnings, we will combine the total compensation of the two physicians and divide by the full-time equivalency. The analysis appears as follows:

Compensation and Excess Earnings Analysis

	1993	1994	1995
Tom Freewilly, M.D.	$120,497	$131,655	$133,592
John Freewilly, M.D.	$108,237	$109,951	$110,042
Total Compensation	$228,734	$241,606	$243,634
FTE	1.5	1.5	1.5
Compensation/FTE	$152,489	$161,071	$162,423
Median Compensation (MGMA)	$112,585	$120,000	$122,000
Excess Compensation	$39,904	$41,071	$40,423
Normalized Excess Earnings (3-year mean)			**$40,466**

Development of the Capitalization Rate
Section 6 of Revenue Ruling 59–60 states:

> In the application of certain fundamental valuation factors, such as earnings and dividends, it is necessary to capitalize the average or current results at some appropriate rate. A determination of the proper capitalization rate presents one of the most difficult problems in valuation.

In the text of Revenue Ruling 69–608, capitalization rates of 15 percent to 20 percent were mentioned as an example. Many appraisers are under the misconception that the capitalization rate must stay within this range. In reality, the capitalization rate must be consistent with the rate of return currently needed to attract capital to the type of investment in question.

There are various methods of determining capitalization rates. Using the built up method of determining a capitalization rate results in a rate as follows:

Capitalization Rate Build Up

"Safe" rate (a)	6.21%
General Risk Premium (b)	7.30%
Small Company Risk Premium (c)	5.10%
Specific Company Risk Premium (d)	12.00%
SUBTOTAL	30.61%
Capitalization Rate (rounded)	31%

Notes for Table 2:

(a) *The Wall Street Journal*, 10-year Treasury Bonds, March 7, 1996.

(b) *Stocks, Bonds, Bills and Inflation 1992 Yearbook*, Ibbotson Associates, difference between total return on common stocks and long-term government bonds from 1926 to 1992.

(c) *Stocks, Bonds, Bills and Inflation 1993 Yearbook*, Ibbotson Associates, difference between total return on small company stocks and common stocks from 1926 to 1992.

(d) See next section on development of the specific company risk premium.

Developing the Specific Company Risk Premium
Determining the risk associated with a specific medical practice requires extensive professional judgment by an independent evaluator familiar with the details of operating

a medical practice. We profiled the practice and compared their performance on several key productivity indicators to offer an informed opinion of the business risks faced and the relative achievements of the three physicians. The measurements of performance are drawn from the data analyzed at the time of the site visit. The standards for comparison are drawn from data assembled by the Medical Group Management Association, publications by *Medical Economics* and the American Medical Association, and from our experience as medical management consultants and appraisers to dozens of similar practices. The risk factors are derived from our proprietary database of appraisals.

Key Indicators of Business Risk/Success

Indicator	Standard	Freewilly	Risk Factor
Overhead as percent of net receipts	58%	41%	+8.50%
Net receipts per physician	$320,000	$280,000	−3.75%
Annual volume of office visits per physician	4,300	5,000	+3.25%
Average age of accounts receivable in days	75	60	+2.00%
Volume of active charts per physician	2,000	2,100	+2.00%
Total Risk Value			+12.00%

To complete the capitalization of normalized excess earnings, we divide the normalized excess earnings by the capitalization rate as follows:

$$\$40,466/31\% = \$130,535$$

Adding the net value to the capitalized normalized earnings produces a conclusion of value.

Capitalization of normalized excess earnings	$130,535
Net asset value at fair market value	$74.6764
Total Value (rounded)	**$205,000**

Method #3: The Replacement Method

The overall purpose in valuing goodwill is to try to answer the question, What would it take to replicate the organization in its current form if we started from nothing? How much would it cost to replace equipment with new and used furnishings? How much would the owners have to lose to develop the cash flow the organization now enjoys?

This method calls for the greatest in professional judgment, and is therefore subject to the widest variation in concluding values. Its primary purpose is to examine the assumptions about the value of the components of intangible assets, and as such it is helpful in contributing to an understanding of stock values when combined with other methods. Tangible and intangible values are rounded for convenience.

John Freewilly, M.D., P.C.
Replacement Method

Estimated Costs to Replace:

Furniture, fixtures, and equipment	$80,000
Recruitment for two mid-career general practitioners	$40,000
Operating capital	$35,000
Operating losses until practice maturity	$100,000
Total Replacement Costs	**$255,000**

Supporting Assumptions for the Replacement Value Method

Furniture, Fixtures, and Equipment: This represents the cost of new furniture, fixtures, and equipment comparable in volume and quantity to the current holdings of the practice. The actual cost may vary if either the amount of furniture or the style of replacement items were to change.

Recruitment of Two Mid-Career General Practitioners: The recruitment costs are estimated at $20,000 each, which is the appraiser's estimate of a typical finder's fee in the current market for general practitioners.

Operating Capital: The cash requirements for operations are estimated to be approximately four weeks cash flow, based on the previous years' net receipts.

Operating Losses Until Practice Maturity: The most volatile component of the replacement cost method is the estimate of operating losses a start-up practice of similar size and specialty might face. The figure offered in this analysis is considered by the appraiser to be a conservative value of $50,000 per physician, estimated to be incurred in the first two years of a start-up. The estimate can vary according to the competition, management skill, physician incentives, and payer mix faced by the new practice.

WEIGHTING OF METHODS

The results of the first method yielded an estimate of net asset value at fair market value, which is carried forward into methods two and three. The results of methods two and three are as follows:

Capitalization of Normalized Excess Earnings plus NAV	$205,000
Replacement Method	$255,000

In the appraiser's judgment, each method has weaknesses and strengths. The capitalization method examines excess earnings that may or may not be transferrable to the purchaser, depending on the decisions buyers and sellers make regarding employment and incentive structures. The recent drop in receivables of the past few months can serve as an argument that future benefits to practice ownership may be compromised. The replacement estimates can vary widely, particularly in examining the projected losses to maturity. The volatility of the replacement method weakens its conclusions in a similar manner as the weakness of other methods.

These limitations seem to be relatively equal, however, which draws us to conclude that the conclusion of value should be based on an equal weighting of the two valuation estimates.

The weighting is applied as follows:

Method	Estimate	Weight	Weighted Value
Capitalization Method	$205,000	50%	$102,500
Replacement Method	$255,000	50%	$127,500
Net Valuation (rounded)			**$230,000**

Reality Check

The conclusion of value appears to be consistent with values negotiated in comparable transactions. If the total value of the practice is $230,000 of which about $75,000 is documented as tangible assets, the remainder of $155,000 may be considered the fair market value of goodwill. That calculation would place goodwill at about 37 percent of net receipts for the last full fiscal year. That is slightly higher than the mean of 33 percent and median of 29 percent for the cumulative averages of the results of the *Goodwill Registry* for the period 1985 through 1995.

At $230,000, the practice has a total value of about $115,000 per physician. This appears to be comparable to median values of $111,751 paid for family practices nationwide over the past five years, according to data from *The 1995 Physician Practice Acquisition Resource Book.*

Certification

I hereby certify that, to the best of my knowledge and belief, the statements of fact contained in this report are true and correct, and this report has been prepared in conformity with the Uniform Standards of Professional Appraisal Practice of The Appraisal Foundation and the Principles of Appraisal Practice and Code of Ethics of the American Society of Appraisers.

Appraisal Associates, Inc.

F

Bibliography

American Medical Association. *Buying and Selling Medical Practices: A Valuation Guide*. Chicago: American Medical Association, 1990.

American Medical Association. *Socioeconomic Characteristics of Medical Practice, 1995*. Chicago: American Medical Association, 1995.

American Society of Appraisers. Seminar: "Appraisal of Small Businesses & Professional Practices, BV 205." Chicago, October 1995.

Beck, Leif. "Goodwill Value Is Here to Stay Despite Rumors," *The Physicians Advisory*, April 1994.

Brown, Ronald. *Valuing Professional Practices and Licenses: A Guide for the Matrimonial Practitioner*. Englewood Cliffs, NJ: Prentice Hall Law & Business, 1994.

Burg, Brad. "Selling Your Practice? Avoid These Tax Traps," *Medical Economics*, October 23, 1995.

Cleaverley, William, et al. *The 1995 Physician Practice Acquisition Resource Book*. Columbus, OH: The Center For Healthcare Industry Performance Standards, 1995.

The Health Care Group. *1995 Goodwill Registry*. Plymouth Meeting, PA: The Health Care Group, 1995.

Institute of Business Appraisers, Inc. Seminar: "Valuing Closely Held Businesses." Denver, May 1995.

Kaiser, C. F., P. D. Haney, and T. J. Sullivan. "Integrated Delivery Systems and Joint Venture Dissolutions Update." *IRS Continuing Professional Education Exempt Organizations Technical Instruction Program (FY 1995).* (1 October): 153–90.

Medical Group Management Association. *Cost Survey.* Englewood, CO: Medical Group Management Association, 1995.

Medical Group Management Association. "Buying, Selling and Valuing a Practice." MGMA Library Resource Center Search Summary Packet, 1995.

Medical Group Management Association. *Physician Compensation And Production Survey.* Englewood, CO: Medical Group Management Association, 1995.

Miles, Raymond. *Basic Business Appraisal.* Boynton Beach, FL: Southeast Business Investment Corp., 1984.

Niswonger, C. Rollin and Philip Fess. *Accounting Principles.* Cincinnati, OH: South-Western Publishing Co., 1977.

Pratt, Shannon. *Valuing A Business, The Analysis And Appraisal Of Closely Held Companies.* Blue Ridge, Illinois: Irwin Professional Publishing, 1981, 1989.

Pratt, Shannon. *Valuing Small Businesses And Professional Practices.* Blue Ridge, Illinois: Irwin Professional Publishing, 1986, 1993.

Rimmer, Timothy. "Physician Practice Acquisitions: Valuation Issues and Concerns," *Hospital & Health Services Administration, The Journal Of The Foundation Of The American College Of Healthcare Executives.* Volume 40, Number 3/Fall, 1995.

INDEX